www.gardenpublishingco.com

SAY FATHER

LESSONS IN SPIRITUAL WARFARE FROM A DELIVERANCE MINISTRY PIONEER

KEN HOWERTON

Copyright ©2019 by Ken Howerton
Published by Garden Publishing Company LLC
For more information, please visit gardenpublishingco.com

All rights reserved. No parts of this publication may be reproduced, stored in a retrieval system, or transmitted in any form or by any means, electronic, mechanical, photocopying, recording, or otherwise, without the prior written permission of the copyright owner.

This book is sold subject to the condition that it shall not, by way of trade or otherwise, be lent, resold, hired out, or otherwise circulated without the publisher's prior consent in any form of binding or cover other than that in which it is published and without a similar condition including this condition being imposed on the subsequent purchaser. Under no circumstances may any part of this book be photocopied for resale.

ISBN 978-0-9966453-9-3
Cover design by Garden Publishing Co./Whitney Whitt
Interior design by Garden Publishing Co.

Printed in the United States of America.

TABLE OF CONTENTS

Foreword from Author	7
Introduction	9
Chapter 1: The Beginning	13
Chapter 2: Growing in Understanding	17
Chapter 3: When God Calls...	21
Chapter 4: The Excitement of the Supernatural	25
Chapter 5: Pressing into the Supernatural	31
Chapter 6: Learning to Walk in Authority	39
Chapter 7: Spiritual Warfare 101: The Battle is Real	47
Chapter 8: Understanding Deliverance	57
Chapter 9: The Process of Deliverance	65
Chapter 10: Always, Always Depend on Holy Spirit	73
Chapter 11: Deliverance Testimonies	81
Chapter 12: Protect Yourself from the Enemy	89
Chapter 13: Cleanse the House	99
Chapter 14: Your Spirit-Led Prayer Makes an Impact	105
Chapter 15: A Lifestyle that Demonstates the Love of God	115
Appendix: Sample Prayers	123

FOREWARD FROM THE AUTHOR

The first experience Carolyn and I had with deliverance was in July of 1981, and as you'll read, the Lord caused such a rapid progression that we were soon receiving twenty to thirty phone calls per day. They came day and night from all over the United States, Canada, the Caribbean Islands, Belize, and Honduras.

Soon, we started getting invitations to teach about deliverance and do mass deliverance sessions, which led to many people asking us if we had ever written a book about our experiences with deliverance and our knowledge of the spirit realm. Some people specifically requested that we write about our experiences and include prayers that people could identify with and use for self-deliverance.

This is where Brandy Helton, Lauren Caldwell, and Kevin McSpadden stepped in to help. They worked together to help me write this book, since I am truly not a writer. What you're reading now is the result of our combined efforts to faithfully represent what God has accomplished through Carolyn and me over many years of walking with Him.

My whole concept for the book is not to entertain you, but to genuinely help each of you. I hope that you will be able to relate your problems to the experiences I have shared. I want this book to teach you how to do self-deliverance so that you can overcome the issues you're facing by the power of God. My prayer for you as you pick up this book is that you will be anointed by the Holy Spirit to seek deliverance so that you may fulfill God's calling on your life.

Father, as I lift up the person who is reading this book and place them boldly on Your lap at the Throne of Grace, I am asking you to supernaturally change the desires of their heart to line up with Your plan for them, which You placed in their spirit from the beginning of time to establish Your Kingdom on Earth as it is in Heaven. Father, I ask You to flood them with supernatural knowledge of Your Word, how it works, and the wisdom to accomplish Your will. Help them to step from the natural realm into the spirit realm in order to fulfill Your Word in John 14:12, to not only do the works of Jesus, but the works that are beyond the comprehension of the human mind, which are the signs and wonders that will bring in multitudes of people into Your Kingdom. I now release the supernatural anointing of Holy Spirit to flow into this reader to step outside the box of the past and into the supernatural walk with Jesus, to do His works in the POWER of Holy Spirit for the glory of our Heavenly Father. In Jesus' name, Amen.

Ken Howerton

INTRODUCTION

Ken and Carolyn Howerton are living proof that sometimes a first impression can be completely, hilariously wrong.

When I first met Ken and Carolyn, they had come to San Angelo at the request of Brandy Helton, apostle and founder of the Garden Apostolic Training Center. At that time, the Garden was in its fledgling stage, and a group of about forty people pursuing the Lord there had gathered for what Brandy called a "group deliverance session." Most, if not all of us, had been through at least a couple rounds of deliverance at that point, and I, for one, thought this day would be a piece of cake. Little did I know how wrong I was.

Despite my erroneous belief that I didn't have much spiritual junk to deal with, I was excited to meet the Howertons. Based on what Brandy had told us about them, I knew they were deep into high-level spiritual warfare. I expected them to be about nine and a half feet tall. I envisioned somber and vicious-looking warriors on a mission to wipe hell from the face of the earth.

So I was a little puzzled when a nice-looking older gentleman and his sweet wife walked into the building where we met, smiling warmly and greeting everyone the way your best friend's grandparents would. While I immediately felt right at home with the Howertons, I must admit I was a tad underwhelmed by their actual presence in light of my extravagant expectations.

That lasted right up until the deliverance session began.

Our group squeezed into the confines of the small-ish room where we had gathered, and Ken parked himself at the front of the group. Carolyn took up her post at his side, and Brandy stood off to the side, smiling because she knew what was about to happen.

Ken flashed his warm smile and spoke for a few minutes about what we would be doing that day. Then, without any fanfare whatsoever, he said, "Now let's get started. Everyone say 'Father...'" And the battle was on.

Now, I thought I knew the people in that room with me that day, but it turns out that wasn't quite the case. I think we all believed we were fairly clean, spiritually speaking, but the Howertons began casting demons out of us left and right. On top of that, people I thought were perfectly decent folks began doing unseemly things like writhing in their chairs or falling to the floor, contorting and screaming. How rude!

While this was happening, Ken and Carolyn mostly took it all in stride. There was no yelling in anyone's face, nor were there any elaborate gesticulations. They just gave simple, direct commands for demons to leave. If the spirits didn't cooperate, the Howertons called on angels to "sack those dumb devils up, jerk them out, and work them over unmercifully." That did the trick, and on we went.

In between casting spirits out, Ken would occasionally get into storytelling mode. He would venture off into some tale about things that happened in the past and before you knew it, someone would inevitably raise their hand and say things like "my stomach feels like it's about to explode" or "I'm getting really dizzy." Who knew a story could cause demons to manifest?

It even happened to me! Throughout the day, I felt odd pains manifesting in my physical body as the Howertons ministered. I felt dizzy at times, inexplicably sleepy and heavy at others, but as spirits left, I immediately noticed a difference. I didn't weigh myself to confirm this, but I continually felt lighter and lighter throughout the day.

Now I know what some of you are thinking, but I'm not a courtesy-fall kind of guy. I don't blow smoke, and I don't do fake. I figure if it's not real, there's no sense acting like it is. You don't get spiritual brownie points for pretending. That day, I expected practically nothing to happen to me, but quite a bit happened anyway, so I knew beyond a shadow of a doubt that what I experienced was real.

As the day wore on, a distinct pattern emerged. Ken would talk, someone would manifest, and Ken would say, "Okay everybody say 'Father, in the mighty name of Jesus...'" Ken would lead us in repentance, receiving forgiveness, and casting out devils by the bucketful. He could rattle off the names of spirits about a dozen at a time. At one point, I wondered how this man could even remember the names of all these devils (As you'll read later, Ken does not actually have the names of spirits memorized – the Holy Spirit reveals them to him). I had never even heard of some of them before, but here he was casting them out of me.

Occasionally, Carolyn would fix someone with a piercing, hawk-like gaze and say, "Ken, there's a spirit of so-and-so in that person." Whoever it was would follow Ken in a prayer if they were able. If not, Brandy or Carolyn would walk over and deal with it, and the deliverance session continued.

At one point, a couple hours in, Ken flashed his smile at us all and said, "I'm so proud of you all. You're doing really well!"

Funny, I thought. *I don't feel like I'm doing well. I feel like a filthy, wet dish rag being wrung out.* We were all fairly exhausted, but none could deny the freedom Holy Spirit was manifesting through the ministry of the Howertons.

By the end of the day, I understood that my expectations and first impressions of Ken and Carolyn were completely wrong. These really were two mighty, vicious warriors ready to take on hell wherever they found it. They exhibited strength and authority the likes of which I have seldom seen in others. At the same time, they exuded such humility and love that I knew in my heart I could trust them completely. Countless times, we watched Ken rise up in fierce authority to cast out high-ranking devils, then weep with tenderness as the Holy Spirit touched him. We laughed along with Carolyn's sassy humor, then stood amazed as she fearlessly fought to set someone free. It was a day to be remembered, and they've given us several such days since.

I tell you that story because I want you to settle this in your heart before you read this book: Ken and Carolyn Howerton are the real deal.

They've been battling the forces of darkness for over thirty years, and they have the scars to prove it. Much like it was said of the first apostles, it is evident that they have been trained by the Lord. Their knowledge has come from intense research and study, along with many years of depending fully on the Holy Spirit in situations that were literally life or death. On top of that, they have a genuine love for the Word of God, and they have received the Father's heart to help people to know Jesus through His Word.

So when you read this book, please approach it with the

understanding that Ken is freely giving you knowledge and revelation that he and Carolyn have spent decades learning. He is offering you the opportunity to fight viciously and live victoriously without having to go through the struggles and setbacks he experienced. This is the testimony of a seasoned veteran in the army of Heaven, and anyone who reads this book would do well to treat it as such.

One word of caution before you continue: if you're not willing to be challenged or stretched, you should put this book down right now. This is not a book for the comfort-loving or the faint of heart. Ken would tell you himself that he fears God alone and doesn't tickle men's ears.

However, if you're ready to rise up to the high call of God to tear down hell and release the Kingdom of Jesus on this earth, fasten your seatbelt and read on. You won't be disappointed.

Kevin McSpadden
Leadership team, Garden Gathering
Church, Author of
Average Christians Don't Exist

CHAPTER 1
THE BEGINNING

I think it's funny and a little sad, but when I say the word "supernatural," the first thing that pops into most people's head is something evil or awful. The church has done such a poor job of teaching people about the realities of the supernatural world that a great many Christians are afraid to engage with it.

But it says right there in your Bible that *"the worlds were framed by the word of God, so that the things which are seen were not made of things which are visible"* (Hebrews 11:3). In other words, there's a far sight more going on in our lives than what we can see with our physical eyes. If you think about it, Christians carry out a number of supernatural tasks every single day.

When a believer prays, he or she communicates with the Maker of the Universe. The Bible describes how a believer has the right to go before the very Throne of Grace to stand in the presence of Almighty God (Hebrews 4:16). Lives are transformed by the very love and grace of God through the power and presence of the Holy Spirit. When the Word of God is released, armies of angels go forth to carry it out. And that barely scratches the surface of the supernatural deeds God has planned for His people.

That's why, whenever I get the chance, I strive to open people's eyes to the power that comes from living in communion with the Holy Spirit. It's not just for the famous or the special; God intends for all of His people to walk in supernatural grace, power, and love.

The truth is the realm of the spirit is all around us all the time. God wants all of His people to know and understand how to walk in this unseen, but real and valid realm because that's the place where His Kingdom operates. Now many people are either unwilling to see it or ignorant that it exists, but it's right there, at finger's touch if we're willing to allow the Holy Spirit to open our hearts to be aware of it. I can even tell of how from a young age He was trying to do that very thing for me.

I was born and raised in the Nazarene church, but that's about as much as I can say about it. I was in it, but it wasn't in me. Nevertheless, even from a young age God was at work in my life. I remember one experience in particular that happened when I was a young boy during World War II. We were living in Gladewater, Texas, at the time, and I was walking down the street with my mother and daddy. As we passed a storefront, I literally saw myself walk through a plate glass window, pass down through the displays, return back out from the window, and continue walking with my parents. And it wasn't until just recently, many years after that happened, that I finally recalled that event. It had been blocked from my mind. But that may well have been one of my earliest encounters with the spirit realm.

For whatever reason, that event must not have had much impact on me because I continued on as I was before. That started to change in 1953, when I met my wife Carolyn and started attending a church in the Assemblies of God. I saw things in that church that I hadn't seen before in the Nazarene denomination, but in some ways it was quite similar. Carolyn and I married in 1957, and at that time I started seeing some real differences.

But during that same time, we had a pastor that did some things to Carolyn that involved being a peeping Tom. So that served to turn me against church for a while. Following that pastor, we had other pastors come in, and one of them kept telling us how fortunate we were to have him as a pastor. I finally told Carolyn I didn't feel the need to listen to that garbage. When that pastor came to our house a few months later, I ran him out of my home, which was completely wrong. However, from that time, we went thirteen years without ever going to church again.

That lasted until April of 1980 when we were invited to a church in Oklahoma City. At that time, I began to sense something I had never sensed before, even though I was a rank sinner. Things were happening in my life which had never happened before. Carolyn had been watching a program with J.R. Church called "Prophecy in the News." That started to get me interested in prophecy. Not long after that, in June of 1980, I accepted Jesus as my personal

Lord and Savior.

At that time I was an engineer at Tinker Air Force Base. I served in the Oklahoma Air National Guard and had logged over 6,200 flight hours. I was a pretty rough character in those days. As a Master Sergeant on flying status, I was the go-to guy in my domain, and you didn't want to cross me. If you did something wrong around me, it didn't matter who you were, I could rip you to shreds with my foul mouth in a matter of seconds and leave you in my dust.

That all changed when Jesus saved me. My life changed immediately in more ways than I could recount in this short space. But one of the first things the Lord did was clean up my vocabulary. And don't think people didn't notice. I got more than one funny look when people realized what a difference it made to have Jesus cleaning up the language coming out of my mouth. That's just one example, too. I guess some would say I was "radically" saved, but I just like to think of it as being truly saved. Jesus has a different definition of radical than we do, and He can make big changes in our lives in a short time. He's in the people-transforming business.

When Carolyn and I got saved, God immediately placed a lady in our lives as a personal teacher of the Bible. She was a powerful believer. When she prayed, the walls rattled with power and authority. We had her as our personal teacher of the Word for about five years, and during those five years, not a day went by without a prophecy or a word in tongues from her. Sometimes there would be two or three times in a single day that she had a word for Carolyn or me.

She was a sign painter and illustrator at Tinker, and her office was in the same building as the machine shop where I spent quite a bit of time. We interfaced quite a bit at work. Either she'd come in to see me, or I'd go in to her office, and a prophecy would spring forth, or tongues would start rolling out of her like a river. Then the Word of the Lord would come to me and relay a message or show me some important piece of information. Sometimes it would even be something specific that I needed to learn, or possibly even preach or teach from the Word. Those five years were like a crash course for me where God showed me what I would need to know in order to accomplish His purpose for my life.

Eventually though, after around five years, the Lord closed

that door. I've never understood why He did not allow us to continue with that powerful lady, but I suppose it's irrelevant. The important thing is that He had laid hold of Carolyn and me, and that we were learning to walk in His ways. We were learning to hear the Holy Spirit in all that we did, not just on Sunday mornings at a church.

Basically, we were just two people minding our own business and loving Jesus the best we knew how. Little did we know how big a plan God had for us.

CHAPTER 2
GROWING IN UNDERSTANDING

I believe God had his eye on Carolyn and me long before we gave our lives to Him. I think that's true of anyone, really, but I remember how the Lord showed Himself to us in such a powerful way long before we were even saved.

It happened in July of 1957, and the short version of the story is that Carolyn and I encountered the love of Jesus in an open vision. It was shortly after we were married and we were playing a round of mini-golf. It was on a perfectly clear evening with a bright sky. Right about the time Carolyn put the ball down, a cloud appeared, about the size of a basketball, and it had what looked like a neon light in it.

As we watched, the cloud became huge, formed into the shape of the cross, and Jesus appeared from the armpit up. He was looking into the north. Then He turned His face to us, and the only way I can describe that face is that it was the most loving face you've ever laid eyes on. Every cell of His body radiates with love. As He looked at us with all that love, He smiled directly at us, then turned to face north again, and no longer appeared to us. Soon enough, the entire cloud disappeared and left the clear sky behind again.

So why did it take me so long to give my life to the Lord after that? I suppose only the Holy Spirit can give a satisfactory answer to that question. Nevertheless, it shows the lengths the Lord will go to as He earnestly reaches out to every person with His love. Not one person is beyond the reach of the love of Jesus Christ, not a single one! I'm living proof.

After we got saved, the Lord continued to work powerfully and diligently in our lives. Even though you might say that we were just beginners in the faith ourselves, the Lord wasted no time in bringing us people who needed our help.

And I want to make that very clear: we never once went looking for someone we could pray for. The Lord has brought literally every single person we've helped to us. It never has been or will be our desire to start a church or some kind of movement unless that's what the Holy Spirit specifically tells us to do. Nonetheless, we've always had the desire to follow Him and do what He says, which I think explains why He started using us to minister to people very early on.

For instance, Carolyn and I had only been saved for about a year when she led a young lady who was a checker at a grocery store to the Lord. Now this young lady had never been to church in her life. Carolyn had told her to get a Bible and start reading it, but that wasn't working out for this young woman. So the Lord told us to go pick her up, bring her to our house, and show her how to study the Word.

At the end of the evening, when we were about to leave to take her home, the Holy Spirit told me to pray for her. When I would pray for people, I would usually put my hand on the back of their necks and pray whatever I felt led to pray, and when I did that to this young lady, out of my mouth supernaturally came the names of six demon spirits afflicting her. Now keep in mind that at that point I had never seen a demon cast out before. I had never read a book on deliverance or anything like it, so I had no knowledge about it whatsoever. To add to that, Carolyn reached up and touched this young lady on the forehead, and she fell down on our floor and started to writhe like a snake!

At the time this all happened I was still a Master Sargent on flying status, so my patience for adults was practically zero. The first thought that came into my mind was to pick this lady up, toss her out the door, and tell her not to ever set foot on my property again. But suddenly, a deep compassion came over me the likes of which I had never before felt for any adult. Carolyn knelt down on one side of the young lady, and I knelt down on the other side, and one by one, we began to cast those demons out.

While this was going on, the most horrible sounds kept coming out of the young woman's mouth, and her face contorted terribly. All the while, she kept right on writhing like a snake, but Carolyn and I kept casting demons out of her as we were led by the

Holy Spirit. When the last one finally came out of her, all she could do was proclaim, "I'm free! I'm free!" She was completely relaxed, and she looked like a 100-Watt lightbulb had lit up her face.

And that was our introduction to deliverance.

From that day, which was in July of 1981, until now, very few days pass by without our casting demons out of somebody. It may be a full-blown deliverance, or it may be one or two spirits at a time, but the Lord has continued to present us with opportunities to set people free from demonic oppression.

During those early years, we continued to grow and learn as the Lord gave us opportunity. We attended a church that could seat 6,000 people, and at almost every service, someone would come to us asking for prayer. Meanwhile, the Lord kept building us up in the deliverance ministry.

Ironically, deliverance was a big no-no in the denomination of the church we attended because their doctrine held that a Christian couldn't have a demon. At the same time, they couldn't understand why people in the church were sick and there was as much sin inside the body of Christ as there was in the secular world. It actually got us in a little trouble with our church leaders. You see they had settled for the doctrine of man rather than listen to the full counsel of the Word of God. Our heart was to listen to and obey the entire Bible, not to pick and choose, but they didn't see it that way.

As we matured, a lot of people kept coming to us for prayer. They would call us or come to our house. Often someone would catch us after church. People would sometimes even pull us out of a church service to come and pray for someone who needed deliverance. Many of the church leaders' family members would come to us, unknown to the leaders, and receive ministry. It got to the point where most of the time after a Sunday night service, Carolyn and I would close the church up. We would often stay long after the leaders had all left for the night, praying and casting out demons.

One day, a pastor came to me, upset because I had been called out of the service several times to go and pray for some people. He told me I should have asked the others to sit down and listen to the sermon before I went and ministered. I simply explained that in this case, the people I was praying for were in such a severe situation that they could not possibly have listened to the sermon. They needed to be delivered before they could truly hear and receive anything he was saying. Needless to say, the pastor didn't agree, and we found ourselves in trouble just for doing what the Lord told us to do.

Unfortunately, that was not the only time such a thing has happened to us as a result of the ministry Jesus gave us. There have been a lot of areas where we have been put down very heavily by the church for ministering deliverance, but we just persevere. We've gone on being obedient and following the Lord where and how He leads us. And when some people didn't like it, we've told them, "Hit the door, Jack, and don't come back." We've been very friendly and cordial, of course, but we refuse to compromise the truth or back off on what we've been given to do simply because somebody doesn't like it.

That may sound harsh, but that's really the kind of attitude a Christian needs to develop. The church has gotten off its mission in many ways because so many believers are more concerned with what their fellow man thinks instead of what God thinks. Deliverance doesn't fit the mold many churches are trying to cram the Holy Spirit into. It's not pretty sometimes, and it takes guts to face the truth that even a believer can have demons operating in and through his life. But what we've found over the years is that God will find a way to show people the truth, whether they like it or not. Once He's shown them, they'll get to decide whether to believe Him or stay hidden in their little comfort zones.

As for us, we choose to follow Holy Spirit. It's a lot more fun that way.

CHAPTER 3
WHEN GOD CALLS...

As I've said, in 1981, the Lord started really building Carolyn and me up in the deliverance ministry. We kept getting opportunities upon opportunities to pray and minister, and the Holy Spirit was constantly growing us and teaching us what we needed to know in order to be effective for His Kingdom.

Years went by and we found ourselves busier and busier with people who needed help getting free from demonic oppression. People with all kinds of sin, sickness, and disease would come to us for help.

By 1985, I was feeling led to take an early retirement from Tinker Air Force Base. At that time, I had already been led to retire from the Air National Guard in order to free up more time for deliverance ministry, but once I heard the call to retire fully, I started gearing all my household finances toward the goal of early retirement.

It took a few more years, but by the grace of God, on January 2, 1988, I was able to completely retire from my engineering position. At that time, I was able to draw out all but 10% of my retirement in order to pay off every debt I had. Now that I was on full retirement status and with all that debt paid off, I made myself available to the Lord 24/7 for whatever He called us to do. From that time on, for a period of about five years, Carolyn and I ministered deliverance around the clock.

You may think I'm exaggerating when I say "around the clock," but that's a pretty accurate description of what we were doing. Sometimes we'd be getting calls around five or six in the morning, and we'd continue until late in the evening. Some days we would minister to people for ten to twelve hours without hanging up the phone. As soon as one phone call would end, there was another waiting. We'd just click over to the new conversation and keep right on going. Our days were really full and God was doing great and mighty works in people's lives.

After a while though, that kind of schedule really starts to wear you down. Eventually, I went to God in prayer and said, "Lord, this is physically wearing me out. I can't keep this up much longer." Immediately, our load was cut to three or four phone calls a day. That may sound like a lot still, but when you're used to twelve or more, it's actually quite a break! Some days there may be more, and some days there are not as many, but now that the calls have diminished a little, they're easier to handle. I can get to them all without feeling worn out, and the Lord continues to bring us people to pray for on a daily basis.

During the same time period that God was growing us so powerfully in deliverance ministry, He also revealed a major part of His purpose for our lives, something bigger than I had imagined.

In November of 1985, Carolyn was playing the part of Mary in a Christmas pageant at the church we attended. I was helping build the stage props when one of the church members who was a prophet contacted me and told me he had a word for me. So during the next practice, I went up to the church, and after the practice was over, we got in my car to talk. The presence of the Holy Spirit filled that car so thickly I thought the windows were going to burst out! Then the prophet gave me the word: "My son, I have chosen you; you did not choose me. The ministry I have chosen for you is my ministry, not your ministry. The ministry I have chosen for you is beyond your comprehension at this time."

I was blown away. I never knew I had *any* ministry. I just wanted to be involved in helps and do what I could to serve people. I was more than happy to be a behind-the-scenes guy! From that time on, though, my whole frame of reference began to change. It was like God was literally changing my mind to prepare me for what He wanted me to do.

One year later, almost to the day, in November of 1986, that same prophet called me again with another word from the Lord. This time He said, "My son the ministry I have chosen for you is the ministry of the apostle. I will keep you in the shadow of my church until the last of the last days. And then I will release you into my church. I will be sending you around the earth to tell my church the error of their doctrine. And they have to make the decision to change, and if they choose not to they will die."

So you see, what God had planned for me was far bigger than I had ever dreamed. And as you can imagine, it wasn't necessarily a fun thing to receive that word. It was actually really hard. But I wasn't about to say no! Since then I've made it my number one priority to simply do what the Holy Spirit tells me to do. If He's not doing it, I leave it alone, whatever it may be or however good it may look.

Since I received that call and continued following the Lord in deliverance ministry, He has far exceeded any expectations I might have had. For over thirty-seven years, Carolyn and I have continued to receive phone calls from all over, most of which come from people we've never heard of.

We've travelled and ministered from California to Pennsylvania, from Canada to the southern tip of Texas. We've prayed with people from at least forty states and three provinces of Canada. We've ministered to people from Belize, Honduras, Nicaragua, and all over North America.

It is really fun when we ask some of these people how they found us and they say, "Holy Spirit told us your name and gave us the phone number." Sometimes they even ask us where we live, and they're amazed when we tell them we live in Oklahoma.

We've had Jewish people call us asking for help. I've asked them how they found me, and they simply reply that the Lord told them to call me. These are full-blown Jewish folks, but I lead them to the Lord and set them free by the Holy Ghost. God's not kidding when He says we have to be ready for anything!

This is a funny story, but one time a lady contacted me who lived in northern New York. We set up an appointment for prayer, and I called her back. I did not realize at the time that her phone number actually came through Canada, so that deliverance actually cost me a hundred and forty bucks, but she got free.

Again, not one of these were people that Carolyn and I hunted down. The Lord brought them all to us. All we did was answer His call.

Say Father

CHAPTER 4
THE EXCITEMENT OF THE SUPERNATURAL

As the Lord continued to grow Carolyn and me in ministry and increase our knowledge of His ways, He began to reveal more and more about how the spirit world operated. God spoke to me one day and said, <u>*"My son, until you understand the function, the operation, and the assignments of the spirit realm, you will never understand the things that go on about you in the natural realm."*</u> Everything that takes place in the natural realm occurs under the direction of the spirit, either the Holy Spirit or demon spirits.

That's one truth that can completely transform the way people live their lives on a daily basis. If people would open their eyes up and let the Holy Spirit make them aware of the ways their natural lives reflect supernatural reality, there definitely wouldn't be as many discouraged, backsliding Christians walking around! On top of that, it would certainly blow away the limits most people have placed on what God can really do in their lives.

With that in mind, the Church must begin to see our walk with Christ Jesus differently than we've ever seen it before. We need to stop putting limits on God and simply believe what God says He can and will do. To truly walk the walk and talk the talk, so to speak, is more fun than anything else I've ever done.

Before I became a Christian, I worked on the kinds of projects that most engineers dream about. I got to invent a lot of things, create processes that had never been done before, and I even did some design work on presidential airplanes. On top of that, as a Loadmaster on flying status, I flew all over the world to some of the best places you could imagine, not to mention some I never care to go again! I joke that many moments of sheer terror are what turned my hair gray.

But the excitement of the walk I have with the Lord Jesus puts all of that to shame.

To illustrate the kind of amazing feats God can accomplish when people surrender to His will, let me tell you about a time I was translated to Russia. It was March of 1986. The pastor of the church Carolyn and I were attending was calling groups of people up for prayer. While this happened, I leaned back and relaxed with my arms over the pew. As a new group of people went up for ministry, I discovered I was no longer in the same church any more. I was in a little church somewhere up in northern Siberia.

I can still describe it in great detail. The walls of this church were twelve to fourteen feet high. The ceiling went up into a peak. The pews reached from the center aisle to the wall and could hold around six to eight people each. The seating filled about three quarters of the church from front to back, and the back third of the pews were empty. At the back of the church, there was an empty space where people could gather and talk. The back wall had wooden pegs where the people had left their coats. As I looked around, I realized suddenly that the doors of the church had swung inward, and I thought that was strange. Normally that would mean someone was about to come in, but I hadn't seen anyone yet.

All at once, about thirty or forty Russian troops wearing full tunic uniforms burst through those doors, all carrying assault rifles. They quickly formed a double row all the way across the back of the church. The soldiers began to level their rifles on the backs of the pews as though they were going to mow the heads off of the entire congregation.

So I pointed right at them and I said, "In the name of Jesus, I command you to drop your weapons, in Jesus's mighty name." It was one sound as the rifle butts hit the floor at the same instant. The men's eyes were about as big around as saucers and their faces were filled with absolute terror. Not fear, terror. There's a difference. I pointed at them again and said, "In Jesus name, I command you men to come up, sit down, be still, and do not move, in Jesus mighty name!" Now those men scurried up into those empty pews and sat at attention, still terrified. Then I said, "In Jesus mighty name I command the warring angels to stand guard over these doors. Let nobody in and let nobody out in Jesus mighty name!"

Just like that, I was back in the church Carolyn and I were attending. Until you have had the experience of being translated, you cannot imagine the power! How did God take me through walls and across thousands of miles in about the same amount of time it took you to read that story? People say it was just my spirit, but I saw my clothes, my shoes, my white shirt sticking out of my jacket. I was totally together. The experience was so overwhelming I couldn't do anything but cry. It took me forty-five minutes just to explain to my wife what had happened.

Later on I was able to share this experience with a friend who sees in the spirit the way most of us watch television. He asked the Lord to show him what it was that had so terrified those soldiers. God showed him that behind me in that church in Siberia, the entire front part of the church was filled with warring angels. These angels were so tall that their backs pressed up against the ceiling, and they each held before themselves a flaming sword. The Lord had opened the spiritual eyes of the soldiers so that the men could see these mighty angelic warriors. I believe that every one of those men got saved that night, and I'm looking forward to meeting them in Heaven.

This is the kind of excitement God desires for those who believe in Him. But again, you have to truly walk the walk and talk the talk. If you're trying to walk in the Kingdom and the secular world at the same time, it will be boring and difficult. You really can't accomplish much that way. That's why so many people backslide – they won't get all the way into the Kingdom. But when you do get all the way in, you'll see the power and glory of God. There's nothing more fun than that!

Not only is God's Kingdom fun, but it will transform you too! Before I got saved, my vocabulary would burn the air with blue flame. If somebody crossed me or did wrong on my airplane, I didn't care what their rank was, I corrected the situation, to put it mildly. I could cuss somebody up one side and down the other and leave them in no doubt whatsoever as to how I felt about them or whatever dumb thing they just did.

But the moment I got saved – right after I said the sinner's prayer – my vocabulary was instantaneously cleansed. I've never used a curse word since that time.

However, I was still smoking like a locomotive! I'd been saved about three months, and my habit was to leave the building after church, head out to the van, and light up a cigarette. Then I'd come stand out front and visit with some of the men out there. So one evening, a lady walked up to me and said, "Holy Spirit told me if I came to you, you'd pray for me and I'd be healed." I was standing there smoking a cigarette! So I took a drag off my cigarette, put my left hand on her, blew smoke in her face, and prayed probably the dumbest prayer God's ever heard. And yet, God healed her!

She probably hadn't gotten three steps away from me when Satan came and spoke in my ear. He told me, "Boy, you're really stupid. Here you are in front of this six thousand seat auditorium and all those people saw you pray for that woman, and she didn't get healed." At least I had enough sense not to acknowledge that I'd even heard him. The same thing happened the next Sunday night, and the following one as well. But by that time, I was ready for him!

So when he came to speak to me, I said, "Satan, I want to thank you. You just confirmed to me that not only was the lady I prayed for tonight healed, but the two previous ladies were also. If they weren't healed, you'd have never said a word, so you confirmed to me that they were healed. Now shut your stupid mouth, and don't you ever speak to me again in Jesus mighty name!" I've never heard his voice since.

Now keep in mind I was still smoking like a steam engine. That lasted from July of 1980 until February of 1982. At that time, an evangelist came in to the church Carolyn and I attended. As he brought the word, he suddenly lowered the microphone, nodded his head, raised the mic again, and said, "There are a lot of you in here tonight that want to quit tobacco." When I heard that, I sprung up out of my seat. The evangelist said about a thirty or forty second prayer, and I was delivered. The spirits of tobacco, nicotine, addiction, habits, and cravings shelled out of me like popcorn because I *wanted* them out. I've never had even a desire for a cigarette since.

After I got delivered, I was still on flying status in the military, and a lot of the guys had heard that I wasn't smoking any more. I got on the airplane one night, and a guy walked right up to me, probably eighteen inches from my face. He said, "Ken I understand you've quit smoking."

I said, "No, God delivered me from cigarettes."

When he heard that, he blew smoke right in my face. It smelled like fresh, cool, clean mountain air. I could not even smell cigarette smoke for about six weeks. I could smell pipe smoke or cigar smoke, but I never smoked any of those. But for about six weeks after that evangelist prayed, I could not smell cigarette smoke. After that, I could smell it, but it stunk horribly bad and I hate the smell of it to this day.

There are so many "little" things like that God has done in our lives. He helps us to help other people. They benefit because of some of the experiences we've had. I can sympathize with people under certain conditions, but there are some that I can't sympathize with because I don't fully understand what they're going through. I can understand to a degree because we've dealt with so many people who have the same or similar issues, but since I've never experienced it for myself, I may not have the complete understanding of the issue. But again, that's where we have to rely on the Holy Spirit to reveal things moment by moment.

It's this kind of supernatural freedom and revelation that will begin to draw multitudes into the Kingdom of the Lord Jesus. I'm beginning to really see strongly how the Holy Spirit is revealing the supernatural to His people. And as he continues to do that, the saints will demonstrate His perfect will and draw all nations to Jesus.

What we're really called to do is reveal Jesus to the world. He gave me a vision early on that revealed to me the reality of being joined to Him in His ministry for His glory.

In the vision, the Spirit took me up and showed me, as though I were looking down from above, a corner section of a field. Now in this field there was a huge oak tree with a trunk probably eight to ten feet in diameter. The field also had a trail running through it diagonally, and it passed under the branches of the huge old oak tree. I saw myself walking from the lower corner of the field toward that tree. I also saw a form that I would describe like a cloud walking toward the tree from the other corner. The form passed under the tree, coming toward me. I saw myself walk into the form. As that happened, the form changed directions and started moving the direction I had been walking. From that moment on, I no longer saw myself, but only saw the form. It was like I had ceased to exist. That was one of the ways God revealed to me the understanding of His Word in Galatians 2:20 when it says, *"It is no longer I who live, but Christ lives in me."*

Throughout our walk with Him, God has been talking to us, and we have made a point of listening. Through experiences like these, the Lord has been and still is raising us up to do the work of

Say Father

His Kingdom.

CHAPTER 5
PRESSING INTO THE SUPERNATURAL

Since the very beginning of my walk, the Lord has worked to open my eyes to the supernatural. I would try to talk to people about what He was showing me, but I discovered that most had no understanding of it whatsoever. Once I figured that out, most of the time when I encountered something of the supernatural realm, I'd just keep my mouth shut and pray and never bring it up. These days, it really bothers me that the church has so much theology that there isn't much common sense or basic understanding. The Word is very simple, but theology complicates it and makes everything into some difficult process or another. Complicating everything builds in so much doubt and unbelief that nobody fully understands what it means to be a supernatural, born-again, spirit-filled tongue-talking, devil-kicking Christian!

It's a shame that even now, when so much has been revealed about the function and operation of the spirit realm that so many believers are afraid to even acknowledge it! But I know beyond a shadow of a doubt that believers should be able to walk through a wall as easily as we walk through a door. We should be able to translate from point A to point B at any time. We should be able to visit Heaven on a regular basis. The Bible says Heaven is our home and we're just sojourners here, so why shouldn't we visit our true home? But we don't do that because we have limited ourselves through a lack of knowledge.

The Bible says *"My people are destroyed for lack of knowledge. Because you have rejected knowledge, I also will reject you from being a priest for Me; Because you have forgotten the law of your God, I also will forget your children"* (Hosea 4:6).

The truth is that we're in a different time frame now, a different concept of life, a different concept of Christianity. As we get ahold of the supernatural, we'll start to see an explosion of the Kingdom of God. Just like the time God translated me to Russia, He will do great feats that many of us have barely imagined. God is able to spread His Kingdom with such supernatural power that none of us could truly comprehend, but that's what will keep the world focused on Him and not us.

The Lord told me one day, "My son, Satan has done a fast and a mighty work, but I shall do a faster and a mightier work than he for I shall do things beyond the comprehension of the human mind." Then He said, "My son, the great oratorical preaching of my Word has not brought in the multitudes of people, but My great signs and wonders will for I shall do things beyond the comprehension of the human mind."

Well, how many people are willing to call those things that be not as though they were (Romans 4:17), especially those things they don't even understand? That's why we've got to allow the Holy Spirit to show us how to walk in the supernatural ways of His Kingdom. Christians in this hour have to be ready to believe for things we haven't even heard of yet.

Let me give you some examples of the kinds of feats God is getting ready to pour out on the church if we will only believe Him.

One day in a vision, I saw the side of a church. It had red brick walls and stained-glass windows, and as I looked at that church, all of a sudden the walls just disappeared. I could see the people inside. I saw that the building had a balcony that covered about the last third of the church. The pulpit was to my right and the balcony was to my left. In the center aisle was a little lady, probably in her sixties or seventies and very frail. Both of her legs were cut off just above the knees. Suddenly, I saw the Lord levitate her up around the level of the balcony, and then He rotated her around that sanctuary three and a half times. As she was being rotated about, I saw her feet and legs grow out. The Lord stood that lady in front of the pulpit on a brand new set of feet and legs.

If that would happen at any church on a Sunday morning, you wouldn't be able to get in there on Sunday night. That's the kind of supernatural that God's getting ready to do among His people.

He also gave me an open vision of a man whose left arm was cut off about three or four inches below the elbow. Holy Spirit said, "My son, command his flesh to cover his spirit." I could see his spirit arm and his spirit hand and fingers sticking out from the stub of his natural arm. So I said, "Father, in the name of Jesus, I command this man's flesh to cover his spirit arm, hand, and fingers." I literally saw his arm, hand, and fingers grow out.

As the body of Christ, we are stepping into a place where we're going to start seeing the limbs grow out. Just look at the number of men and women from Iraq and Afghanistan that have had their limbs blown off. We had a lot of that in Vietnam, but not near the numbers we're seeing now because of the improvised explosive devices (IED's) the enemy is using. Literally hundreds of our troops come home with missing limbs from these IED explosions, and we Christians just happen to serve the King who can make them whole again.

So it's time for the body of Christ to step into the supernatural and quit walking this simple, natural process that we've walked for centuries. We must come out of the ages where the church has been so wimpy, and start living the life of supernatural faith in God. That's what it will take to see the kind of supernatural healings and signs we're talking about here, and that barely scratches the surface of all God will do in our midst.

For example, what kinds of miracles do you suppose the Lord will perform to get the gospel spread to the entire world? Now, you may have been told that Jesus could come back at any moment. That's not true because the Word tells us that Jesus will not return until the gospel has been preached to every living thing. At the present time, only about fifty percent of the world population has never even heard the name of Jesus, let alone the full Gospel.

Once, I flew for eight straight hours from Bogota, Colombia, to Bolivia, and I only saw a couple clearings in the forest as I flew. In those clearings I could see huts and villages in these remote places. We know those jungles are full of people, millions of them. Yet they have no television, no radio, no newspapers, and no education whatsoever. They have no way of hearing the Gospel.

So as I was praying about it one day asking God how He would get the Gospel to those people, especially when nobody knows where they are, the Lord gave me an open vision. In the vision, there was a clearing like the ones I saw on my flight. There were three huts built about eight feet above ground, and three families lived there. They were gathered around a campfire cooking the evening meal. The adults had on basically loincloths, and the children were practically naked. All at once, a white man just appeared in the middle of the clearing on the other side of the fire. He preached the Gospel to those people, and every one of them was saved, baptized in the Holy Spirit, delivered of demon spirits, healed and restored. Then the man who appeared was gone.

I had received the answer to my question.

Even in the more civilized nations we can expect to see this kind of manifestation of God's glory. Years ago, God said to me, "My son, there is a day coming where you'll be able to speak to a large group of people just a few words, and every person will be saved, baptized in the Holy Spirit, delivered of demons, healed, and restored in just a few moments of time." If that's not exciting, I don't know what is.

I've even had personal prophecies that point me to my particular part in the kind of things God is getting ready to do. I had an aunt who had an open vision where Carolyn and I were ministering in the streets with thousands of people. All around us supernatural signs and wonders were happening. Through it all, we were bringing people into the Kingdom.

These kinds of prophecies can be very encouraging. Whenever those visions or words come, it stirs your spirit man and gives you encouragement to go on. Sometimes pressing into the supernatural can become discouraging, especially when you're doing what the Lord has told you to do and people who call themselves Christians come and attack you for it! They can say evil things about you or try to discredit you. That's why the Bible says in Luke 6:22-23, *"Blessed are you when men hate you, And when they exclude you, And revile you, and cast out your name as evil, For the Son of Man's sake. Rejoice in that day and leap for joy! For indeed your reward is great in heaven, For in like manner their fathers did to the prophets."* We have to lay hold of that and keep following where the Holy Spirit leads. And in the meantime, we allow what God speaks to us through His people by way of encouragement to lift us up in our spirits, and we keep pressing forward!

It's becoming clearer and clearer that God is ready to open up a new level of revelation for His people to carry to the world. But if you look at the average church today, what do they have that the average person with any money at all would want? Not to be rude, but if you walk into most churches, most of the people look like they've been dipped in pickle juice. There's no life. There's no power. All they do is whine and cry to God. Those on the outside don't have to look that hard to see all kinds of sin in the congregations. By and large, there's not much going on inside the church to make unsaved people want to be there.

Not only that, but many of the pastors, evangelists, and prophets that call me for deliverance are involved in alcoholism and drug addiction. Many of them are having affairs with members of the church. They're into pornography and even sex with children. These things are sickening to the Lord and they're robbing the church of its power!

In 1981, the Lord told me, "You're going to start seeing pastors drop dead behind the pulpit because they are not teaching My people truth." I believe we're on the edge of that right now. The days of God winking at the sin that is in the church are over. We've hit the end of the chain, so to speak. And yet, the most power that the church has ever experienced is also at our doorstep.

For example, I personally believe that a transfer of finances is getting ready to happen in the church. Some of it will be in natural ways, but much of it will be from supernatural means. I believe we will come to a place where the finances of the entire planet will be in the hands of the body of Christ and we will dictate to the nations how those finances are spent. There will be no more spending for homosexuality or lesbianism or abortions – all of those sinful things that the nations have legalized, so to speak. One of the problems we have in governments today is that they're either promoting sin or legalizing sin. Whenever a nation does that, that nation will fall. Every great nation that has risen and fallen has fallen because of sin. It wasn't just because of bad decision making or some kind of failure to govern. It was because of the sin in that nation. And it would benefit the church immensely to stop viewing the government as the answer to the problems our world faces. We need to return to a dependence on and trust in God as the only real solution.

After all, the Lord is fully capable of financing every single need for His purposes at this precise moment. The Lord told me in the early 1980s, "My son, I know where there is enough lost and hidden treasure to finance the entire ministry for the end days." I don't think He told me that just to entertain me, but I have not yet been told where any of that treasure is located! I do have a desire to get a metal detector, ask the Lord where He wants me to start, and start hunting it. I have an idea of a location that I'll be checking out some time.

Once, we were in Stillwater at an evening meeting, and I was praying over finances. As I was praying, the Lord was showing a lady in attendance an open vision. In the vision, we were driving down a dirt road toward a mountain. There was a barbed wire fence, and as we got close to the fence, the power that was with us blew that fence completely away. Then as we got closer to the mountain, there was another fence with iron bars and brass gates. As we got near, the gate blew away and the iron bars went flying through the air. As we got even closer to the mountain, there was a huge boulder, bigger than a bus, right in our path. But as we approached it, cracks started to form in it, and then it literally crumbled into small rocks, then turned to dust and blew away.

Now behind that huge boulder, there was a cave entrance. As we entered the cave, the lady having the open vision saw demons screaming, ranting, raving, and cussing at us because we were coming into that cave. As we went deeper into the cave, she began to see stacks of gold, silver, platinum, and all kinds of precious metals. Then she started seeing diamonds, rubies, and all kinds of precious stones – stacks, mountains of them in there! As we went even deeper, she started seeing artifacts, art, paintings, sculptures, and so forth.

The Lord showed her this to tell us the magnitude of the treasure Satan has stolen from humanity and hidden. I fully believe God is preparing to release these stolen treasures back into the hands of His people, along with greater and greater release of His awesome power.

When you hear the kinds of things we're talking about here, you can't help but be encouraged. It stirs my spirit to think of all the amazing ways God can reveal (and is revealing) His Kingdom on this earth. Ultimately, His plan has never changed: the church's mission is to be fruitful, multiply, and take dominion here on Earth. By the way, the Bible backs all of what I'm saying here.

So it's time for us to recognize that we must change how we've thought about the Word, along with the way we operate in the Word. It's got to come to the point where the Word is a living part of our lives, 24/7. Once we do that, we're going to see the church changed to a place where people have a desire to be a part of it. When we lay hold of all the Lord has for us, we will literally become the solution to the problems plaguing so many in this world. They'll run to the church, rather than running from us.

Say Father

CHAPTER 6
LEARNING TO WALK IN AUTHORITY

If the Church of Jesus Christ is going to take up its God-given call to manifest His Kingdom here on the earth, then Christians had better start learning to operate in the authority He has given us to do that. Too many church-goers are caught up in the mindset that all there is for them to do is occupy a pew on Sundays, read the Bible, and pray. I'll tell you right now, that's not going to cut it when the battles we're about to see really get started.

I'm not saying that going to church and reading the Bible are bad. I'm simply pointing out that reading the Bible isn't going to do you any good unless you believe what it says about you and you start to enforce that truth in your life and in the world around you. Unfortunately, the missing piece of this equation is that too many Christians don't understand *how* to operate in that kind of dominion. It's simply not taught in many of our churches.

I'm grateful to say the Holy Spirit has opened my eyes to a great many things that are not taught in the modern day church. One of the most important truths He has shown me is what I know as the line of authority, or the chain of command in the spiritual realm. Until someone really understands this concept, they cannot fully understand who they are in Christ Jesus.

Part of the confusion has happened because of some misunderstandings or even misinterpretations of the Word of God. For instance, in Genesis 1:1, the original text does not say, "In the beginning, God created the heavens and the earth." What it says is, *"In the beginning, Elohim, the Aleph and Thav, created the heavens and the earth."* If you do a quick search on this word, you'll discover that Elohim refers to a plural, and yet it is the name God chose with which to describe Himself at creation. Notice that in Genesis 1, God says "*Let us...*" each time He's getting ready to create. Taken together, this establishes that Jesus, as the Living Word of God, and the Holy Spirit were creating with and alongside God the Father. And so the trinity, Father, Son and Holy Spirit, were mentioned from the very beginning.

Continuing that line of thought, consider Psalm 8:5, which many translations misinterpret as saying that man has been made a little lower than the angels. That word for "angels" is "Elohim" in the original text. We now understand that to mean that man was made a little lower than the "Elohim," or a little lower than Father, Son, and Holy Spirit. That changes the way we begin to think about our authority. In fact, if we line it out properly, we discover that redeemed man has a much higher level of authority than many people believe.

With that in mind, this is what Holy Spirit taught me about the true chain of command in the spirit world. At the very top of the order, we have God the Father, Jesus Christ, and Holy Spirit. Right beneath them ranks redeemed man. After redeemed man come the angels in all their rank and order. Then comes Satan, followed by the fallen angels in all their rank and order, demon spirits, and at the very bottom, with no spiritual authority whatsoever, comes fallen man. So that means that redeemed man ranks fourth in spiritual authority, above the angels, not beneath them.

That's why in Hebrews 1:14, it says of the angels, "*Are they not all ministering spirits, sent forth to minister for them who shall be heirs of salvation?*" That tells us that angels minister for us according to the will of the Father. This should start to change the way you understand the spiritual authority God has given you if you are a believer in Jesus.

However, Satan has been very clever in the way he has worked in the church to keep us from knowing our authority in Christ Jesus. Once we truly understand who we are, Holy Spirit starts revealing to us how we are to rise up to destroy the works of the devil. The thought of an army of redeemed men and women who know who they are in Jesus terrifies the enemy. That's why he works so hard to keep us ignorant of our real identity and authority.

Holy Spirit taught me powerfully concerning my spiritual authority in September of 1988. There was a hurricane called "Hurricane Gilbert" approaching the Texas coast at Brownsville.

At that time there were two prayer groups from Houston, Texas, who would watch the developments on the news and call me each time there was an update so we could pray. For three to four days I kept getting these requests for prayer, and I kept watching on television to see what would happen. There was absolutely no change.

Finally I sat down and prayed, "Father, you've got to teach me how to pray the effective and fervent prayer of a righteous man (James 5:16) concerning this hurricane because I see no change." The revelation He gave me came in the form of this answer: "My son, pray a shield of Jesus between the waters and the winds, that the spirits of Poseidon, Leviathan, Neptune, and Hercules cannot rise up out of the sea and give strength, power, and acceleration to the demon spirits of hurricanes, tornadoes, high winds, destructive winds and killer winds. Now my son, dispatch your warring angels into the storm to destroy it."

Notice that the Holy Spirit said "your" warring angels, not "My" warring angels. So I did what the Spirit told me to do, and I was amazed and elated at that kind of prayer because I could feel the power. And God wasn't finished. He then said, "Now my son, pray my word, Exodus 22:18." So I kind of prayed that word flippantly: "Father, Your Word says in Exodus 22:18, '*Thou shalt not suffer a witch to live.*' So Father, I now release Your Word to do its work according to Your will, as you direct by Your Holy Spirit for Your glory." Immediately, in the spirit, I saw five witches drop hammer-dead behind a stone sacrificial altar. I saw another witch drop dead behind her kitchen sink. I saw them as clearly as I've ever seen anything in my life.

Seeing this happen, I began to weep. I prayed, "God, I don't want to be responsible for the deaths of anyone who hasn't had a chance to receive Jesus as their Lord and Savior." The Holy Spirit responded right away, "My son, only those who have committed the unpardonable sin or who have hardened their hearts so that they will never receive Jesus as Lord and Savior will die and they need to be removed because they are a hindrance to My people." So I went from crying to laughing.

Since that time, He has had me pray that prayer I have no idea how many times. I've never seen another person die, but it is our responsibility to release the word the Holy Spirit gives us, and then God can do with it as He pleases.

But to finish the story, after I prayed the way the Holy Spirit led me, I finally saw the change I had been believing for all along. The hurricane suddenly turned as if on a dime and headed into lesser populated areas of Mexico, losing power as it went. You may say that was just coincidence, but I know better.

Not long after things started to change for the better, one of the ladies I'd been in contact with in Houston called me to share what the Holy Spirit had allowed her to see. As the hurricane was heading inland, she saw three huge angels standing on Mountains between the Gulf coast and Monterrey, Mexico. Each of these angels carried huge swords, and they were batting that hurricane with the flat of their swords. As they struck the hurricane, she saw the winds drop down from it like shards of glass.

Now keep in mind that before we prayed, Hurricane Gilbert was moving north, predicted to make landfall at Brownsville with winds of over 200 miles per hour. That would have made it the storm with the highest recorded winds of the twentieth century. But when the Lord showed us how to pray, that storm turned ninety degrees and went into much less populous areas.

I'm sure there were a great many people praying about that storm, and I believe every prayer made some kind of difference. But when the Holy Spirit taught me to pray with such authority and power according to His will, and even a hurricane obeyed what I prayed, that was some of the most overwhelming knowledge He's ever given me! From that time on, I've learned to ask the Holy Spirit to teach me to pray the effective, fervent prayer of a righteous man over just about anything I'm facing. And when you see the authority God has placed in your hands, it sets you down on your knees in a heartbeat.

So that's how the Lord began to teach me about the authority He has given redeemed Man. Many of us have been taught all our lives that God can do anything. Contrary to that notion, God has limited Himself as to what He will do because He gave man dominion on this earth in Genesis 1:28. We're the ones who have authority on this planet. With an understanding of the authority He gave us, we realize that we're the ones who have to "call things that do not exist as though they do" so that God can do what He wants to do.

The Lord gave me what I call the "circle of prayer." Whenever the Father wants something done, He tells the Lord Jesus. Jesus tells the Holy Spirit, and the Holy Spirit confirms to us the Father's will and works with us to pray the Father's will right back to the Father.

Now remember, we're literally praying from a seat in Heaven because we're in Christ Jesus (Ephesians 2:6). If people could actually understand that we're really living in two places – heaven and earth – at the same time, they could grasp the overwhelming power God has given us.

We must speak the will of the Lord by faith in order to receive. However, that same law of faith is the law that allows witchcraft to work. Just as our words of faith release the power of God on Earth, the words of the ungodly empower Satan to exercise his will on Earth. Just as God has limited himself on Earth, Satan cannot do anything on earth either until it is spoken from the mouth of man. That highlights why it is so important to hear and release God's Word in this world. He set us in a place of authority, and we must use that authority to see His will manifest. Furthermore, if we're not going to occupy that place of authority, then Satan's forces will. Releasing God's Word is not just a possibility – it's a necessity.

Now it will be absolutely wonderful when Jesus returns and takes total dominion. Then we won't have to deal with such things as the enemy and his agents anymore. But until that happens, it is the saints who are responsible to express with our mouths by faith, under the direction of the Holy Ghost, those things that proceed from the heart of God.

The key here is to listen to God and obey what He has said. That's where our authority comes from and that's how we will learn to walk in it – by obeying Him in all things. That includes answering the specific and wonderful calling God has placed on your life. There are many out there who have either ignored their call or flat refused it, and I can tell you the end will not be good for those people. The Lord gave me a vision once of the White Throne of Judgment, and it was an extremely chilling experience.

In the vision, it was as though I was sitting on a bleacher about six feet above ground level. Right in front of me, about twelve feet away, there was a line of souls stretching into infinity to the right and to the left. You could not see the end of the line in either direction. Every person in the line was stark naked. In front of them and right in front of me was the White Throne. You cannot imagine how bright and how white the light is at that Throne.

Nothing could possibly hide there. Every one of the people in the line was bent over at the waist with their heads bowed. From their fingertips and thumbs came a stream of blood trickling out. The Lord spoke to me and said, "My son, these are those whom I have called into the fivefold ministry who have refused my call, and this is the blood I will require at their hands." I started crying and said, "Lord, I don't care what you ask me to do, I'm not going to stand in that line."

So from that time, if people can't handle what I'm doing in ministry or what I'm teaching, it doesn't make a bit of difference to me. I refuse to stand in the line God showed me. I am going to obey the Lord, whether anybody else likes it or not. At times, I've stopped in the middle of teaching and said, "I recognize that there are those here who cannot handle this kind of teaching. So hit the door and don't come back until you can." It may sound mean to you if you're operating in the fear of man, but I'm not going to back off from what the Holy Spirit has told me to do. We are not living in a time when God is winking at sin. He is telling us what to do, and whatever He has told us to do is important in His sight. We may not always recognize or fully understand the importance, but that doesn't get us off the hook for disobeying whatever He's asking of us in the moment.

To summarize, the revelation of the spirit realm is accelerating at a pace the world has never seen before. I cannot even verbalize some of the things I sense in my spirit man because it is beyond our capability to understand at this time. But I believe God puts those things in our spirit before we understand what it is and how it works. He puts it in us as a way to prompt us to begin researching it and praying about it. We begin to ask the Lord to show us where this fits into His plan, where it fits into our ability to minister to His people. As He teaches and we begin to understand, we can begin to call those things that be not as though they were in ways most people have never heard of.

Once we gain this kind of knowledge, we will be able to step into the realm that will bring in the multitudes of people. So from now on, let's take a new step and a new route. Let's allow the Holy Spirit to build His authority in us, and let's choose to obey Him regardless of the cost. I believe it's going to be more than worth it. What is before us is wilder than anything we've ever experienced, and I personally can't wait to see what the Lord has in store!

It will be absolutely wonderful when Jesus returns and takes total dominion. Then we won't have to deal with such things as the enemy and his agents anymore. But until that happens, it is the saints' responsibility to express with our mouths by faith, under the direction of the Holy Ghost, those things that proceed from the heart of God.

Say Father

CHAPTER 7
SPIRITUAL WARFARE 101: THE BATTLE IS REAL

Carolyn and I went to a Norvel Hayes conference in 1988 that had a profound impact on our ministry to this day. At this conference, one of the speakers was a young man who shared his testimony of deliverance.

From the time this man was eight until he was twenty-one years old, he had been practicing homosexuality. As a child, he was molested by another homosexual man, which led to severe oppression. He tried and tried to refrain from homosexuality, but was unable. Eventually he made the decision that something had to happen quickly, so he went to talk to his pastor. The pastor told him he had heard of a man named Norvel Hayes who dealt with these kinds of issues.

The pastor drove the young man to Norvel Hayes's home. Norvel took the young man and began hammering the spirit of homosexuality. Through these prayers, the young man got free from homosexuality. What he shared at the conference, though, was that he had made up his mind that if he didn't get free that day, he would kill himself that night. Obviously God had different plans. At the time of the conference, the young man was married and had three daughters.

This man who had gotten so powerfully delivered shared two statements at the conference in May of 1988 that completely permeated my being. First, he said, "You have to know your enemy as well as you know your Savior." Then he said, "Quit telling Jesus about your problems, and start telling your problems about Jesus."

You see, the church as a whole has whined and cried to God to do things for them that is actually their responsibility to do. I've noticed that everything in the Word comes full circle. In the process of telling Jesus about their problems, most Christians whine and cry and ask God to do things that are their responsibility. They have to make the decision to obey God's Word and pray in faith and authority so that God can do His part. I don't know about you, but I've noticed that every time there is a requirement on our part, God does not do His part first. We must do our part first, then God will do His part.

But returning to the first statement the young man at the conference made, it is clear that the church has failed to truly understand who our enemy is and how he operates. That has led to some serious, even fatal, results among a body of believers who are supposed to be victorious and blessed.

So let me make something crystal clear: the time for closing our eyes and pretending that spiritual warfare doesn't exist is over! It never should have started in the first place, but many Christians don't like the thought of demons, so they deny that demons exist or choose not to learn about how to effectively war against them. That's complete foolishness! You wouldn't go to a battlefield and pretend there was no opposing army. That would get you killed in a hurry. So it doesn't make sense for people who believe what the Bible says to go on ignoring the fact that we're in a spiritual war.

We currently operate in a time of warfare the likes of which no person in history has experienced, nor could they have experienced. In recent years, there has been a release of the demonic against the body of Christ far greater than we've ever known. The war is on and people had better get ready for it. They had better allow the Holy Spirit to teach them how to be effective in it, or else they'll go on engaging in ineffectual strategies and not seeing the victory the church is called to walk in.

For example, I've heard people stand in the pulpit and say, "I bind you Satan, in the name of Jesus." Satan just laughs. What the people doing this don't realize is that Satan is not the enemy they're combatting in that moment. He's not the one at work. In the military, in times of war, the enemy is not the general or the head of the nation you're fighting, the enemy is the one across the line shooting at you! So to be effective, you have to deal with the level at which you're being confronted.

Believe it or not, there are many levels of warfare. Deliverance ministry is actually one of the lowest levels of warfare, and the church is scared spitless of deliverance! What are they going to do when they start getting confronted by the princes and powers in the heavenly places? What will they do when they're dealing with fallen angels who have tremendous authority and power?

You see, Satan is the god of this world, and those princes and powers are under his authority. We need proper understanding of how to fight if we're going to defeat these higher level enemies. It takes a government to overthrow a government, or a kingdom to overthrow a kingdom. So, the Kingdom of God has got to be established on this earth, because Satan is the god of this world.

Of course the church as a whole does not seem to understand the difference between "world" and "earth." The word "world" refers to the social system. Unfortunately, the social system of the world has taken over the church. So if you want to get to the bottom line, Satan is actually the head of most of the denominations now. Many people will be offended by what they just read, but that's not my problem. The mandate of the body of Christ is to establish God's Kingdom on the earth to displace the governing authorities and powers Satan has set up through the world systems. We are to be the overtakers, not the overtaken.

For that to happen, the body of Christ has got to come into a new level of discipline that we have not had up to this point. The body as a whole has been basically a bunch of wimps. We can't afford to be undisciplined wimps in the times in which we're living.

I like to say, "A good fight every day keeps your blood churning." It keeps you young. Besides that, it's fun! When you come up against a fight in the spirit, think to yourself, "Well here's a good challenge! Let's get it on!"

And don't think this is just an analogy either. When I say "fight" I mean it! The Lord has given us tremendous revelation in the <u>function</u>, <u>operation</u>, and <u>assignments</u> of the <u>spirit realm</u>. When you start looking at the demonic structure – Satan's kingdom – it's set up like a military. If you looked at military manning documents, it's exactly the same setup. When we understand that, it empowers the way we pray to see people set free from Satan's power.

So what does the enemy army look like?

Satan is at the head. Then there are four fallen angels over the North, South, East, and West. The earth is broken into regions, then nations, then states. States are further divided into quadrants, then counties, cities, and blocks. The structure continues down into individual homes and even individual people. Each person has a controlling and ruling spirit ruling over them.

Furthermore, demons rule from the inside, not the outside like many people think. In order to really set someone free, we have to disconnect them from the ruling spirit that is over them. Then we can cast out the demons at work inside them. We'll dive into this more in later chapters.

It's also important to understand that demons operate in family groups. For example, the spirit of anger is not just anger alone. Along with anger, there are hate, rage, murder, violence, and vindictiveness. Then, there are spirits kindred to them, plus spirits that operate with and through them. Finally, there may be spirits that are tied to them. But the good news is that you may deal with one stronghold but really cast five levels of spirits out of someone at one time!

Learning this took time. Carolyn and I went through a period of about ten to twelve years where we had to query every demon spirit we cast out. We got so tired of talking to demons we could hardly see straight! But we learned things that most people don't have a clue about.

The Lord is so smart! As we were querying these spirits, He never had us *ask* them anything. God directed us to *command* them to tell us what we wanted to know. Of course many times as we were querying them, the demons would get belligerent or refuse to talk. Sometimes they even lied to us, but the Spirit of Truth in us would quicken us to know when they were lying. Holy Spirit also began to reveal to us that we had some mighty allies in the spiritual fights we engaged in – the angels!

Awhile ago, a pastor from Colegate, Oklahoma, went to Cuba on a mission trip. When he came back stateside, he became deathly ill. They put him in the hospital and performed test after test, but the doctors couldn't figure out what was wrong with the man. Meanwhile his condition became worse and worse.

Pretty soon, the pastor's sister and wife called me on the phone and told me what was happening. They asked if I would pray for the man, and of course I prayed for him on the phone. As I prayed, the Holy Spirit told me to call on the Seraphim to take a coal from the Throne of Grace and place that coal on the pastor's lips and belly. When I was praying that, the pastor said he could feel the coal being applied. It burned like fire, he told me, but it didn't hurt a bit!

That moment was when the shift occurred. Up to that point, the doctors had predicted the pastor would die from whatever had been afflicting him, but the man ended up going home perfectly healthy the very next day.

That story highlights something the Holy Spirit has been emphatic about as He has taught me about the supernatural: we need to learn how to interface with the angelic. Psalm 103:19-21 describes how the angels listen for those who are speaking God's Word so that they can carry out His will: "*19 The Lord has established His throne in heaven, And His kingdom rules over all. 20 Bless the Lord, you His angels, Who excel in strength, who do His word, Heeding the voice of His word. 21 Bless the Lord, all you His hosts, You ministers of His, who do His pleasure.*" Do you see that? These angelic forces are waiting to hear someone speaking the Word of God so that they can show up and carry it out! They're searching high and low to find someone who will agree with God's will and His ways so that they can unleash their phenomenal power to see God's will done.

Guess what that means for you and me? We're the ones who get the privilege of listening to the Holy Spirit and releasing God's Word and His will. When we do that, we can expect to see fruit. But you have to, and I mean have to, listen to the Holy Spirit. Otherwise you'll accomplish a whole lot of nothing.

For instance, the Holy Spirit told me we need to be inviting the Seraphim to bring a coal and place it on our lips to cleanse us, to purify us to become what God has called us to be. Most people don't have a clue that we can utilize the angels that God has *already* sent us, let alone call on Seraphim, which are very high ranking angels, to come and minister to us!

But the Lord has made great multitudes of angels available to Christians to help us establish His Kingdom.

Returning to the story about the hurricane, after I prayed the way the Spirit had led me, I thanked the Lord for the 12,000 angels He had sent to me to minister for me. Holy Spirit immediately came back at me and said, "My son you have access to the same number of angels Jesus had access to when he went to the cross." If you understand the Scriptures, you realize that number is more than 72,000. God has already sent those angels to us to minister for us (Hebrews 1:14). Therefore, we must realize that we can't do our part to establish His Kingdom on the earth until we learn to effectively utilize what He has sent to us.

As I have previously discussed, we have a war on our hands that is beyond comprehension. If people could see in the heavenly places and witness the war that's going on, they'd be scared spitless. But that doesn't change the fact that God has placed us into a position of extraordinary authority in the midst of that war. Our place in it is essential.

It's up to us to establish routes to Heaven, to open portals to heaven, and to shut down and seal off Satan's portals. For example, the Holy Spirit showed me that the oil spill in the Gulf of Mexico was an open portal to release demons. When events like that occur, it's up to the church to stand in its authority both to shut off Satan's access to the world and release the dominion of Heaven.

If we're going to do that effectively, we need to get more revelation of the angelic host of heaven. We need to understand how the angels work and how to interface with each one. We must regularly ask the Holy Spirit to show us the strength of each kind of angel, what their purposes are, and how to effectively utilize each one for the glory of the Lord. We have so much to learn!

Even if we only press into the specific types of angels mentioned in the Bible, there will be such a magnitude of knowledge released. And even what we see in the Bible is limited compared to the fullness of what is really out there.

The Lord spoke to me one day, "My Son, My Word the Bible is like the checklist on your airplane, but My Holy Spirit is like the Tech Order Library on your airplane." Now this doesn't mean much to most people, but to explain, the Tech Order Library on a C-130 airplane like the one I was flying on at the time fills a fairly good-sized room with books from floor to ceiling around the entire perimeter and down the center of the room. Every item that airplane is manufactured from is listed in that tech order, along with the formulas and everything else pertaining to that plane. It is a treasure trove of information.

The checklist for the C-130 told me the bare essentials that were necessary to operate that aircraft. The Tech Order Library was the encyclopedia that contained every detail about every single part of that plane. The Holy Spirit knows every detail about the operation of the Kingdom of Heaven, and we could (and will) spend an eternity learning about that operation from Him.

So it is important to rely on the presence of the Holy Spirit in our everyday decision making, what we say, and what we believe. We must rely on Him completely for everything.

John 16:13 says, "*13 However, when He, the Spirit of truth, has come, He will guide you into all truth; for He will not speak on His own authority, but whatever He hears He will speak; and He will tell you things to come.*" It is the Holy Spirit's job to lead us into all truth, and He's good at His job. It follows that if we're really going to learn about the angels, we're going to have to query the Holy Spirit. A good place to start is to ask Him, "Holy Spirit, teach me to utilize the host of angels you have sent to me. You've given me more than 72,000, and I need to learn how to interface with them. Teach me how to speak the words out of my mouth that will place the angels into their needed effect in order to accomplish your purposes and to set people free."

I'll say right up front that my understanding of angels is very limited, even though I've been dealing with and learning about angels for around thirty years. But it is essential to understand that there are angels for every part of our lives. There are angels of mercy, angels of surgery, angels of electronics, and even angels of explosives. There are literally angels for everything you can imagine that pertains to this life. You need to ask the Holy Spirit to teach you to confidently command and direct the angels assigned to you according to God's will. They're at your beck and call to help you, to assist in whatever it is you're called to do, so as you learn to interface with the angels, you'll see more of their ministry manifest.

With these truths in mind, it's easy to see that angels have a tremendous role in deliverance ministry. For example, why do we call on Michael? Why do we bind demon spirits and fallen angels with the chains of Jesus, or call on warring angels to bag them up? These things are all found in Scripture, and the Lord has shown us how to effectively operate with the angels in this way.

Scripture has authorized Christians to call on the angels to help do the work of the Kingdom. Hebrews 1:14 says that the angels are "***all*** *ministering spirits sent forth to minister for those who will inherit salvation?*" (emphasis added). That means we have access to and authority to employ all of them as directed by the Holy Spirit.

We use the chains of Jesus mentioned in Revelation 20:1,

which refers to an angel coming down with a great chain and a key to lock Satan up for a thousand years. So we charge angels to bind fallen angels and demon spirits in the chains of Jesus so that they cannot escape.

The Bible shows that believers have authority to call on even the highest ranking angels. Daniel 12:1 refers to Michael, and says that Michael will deliver all the saints whose names are written in the book. That's why we call on him to come and fulfill that word as we pray deliverance. Lastly, Job 14:17 describes transgression being "*sealed up in a bag*." So we have no problem dispatching angels to sack up and pull out the demons operating through transgression in people's lives.

Once more, I must remind you that all of this comes by revelation of the Holy Spirit, and we do it as He leads.

I want to address an issue concerning calling on Michael. We know that we have the authority to call on him, but it's important to recognize that Michael cannot be at more than one place at a time. He is not omnipresent the way God is. That means that it will probably not be Michael himself assisting in deliverance, but one under his authority. We address Michael as the headship of the warring angels, and he assigns whatever warring angels we need to assist us.

It's similar to the process of addressing an Embassy. Whenever anyone addresses a U.S. Embassy in foreign countries, they are literally addressing the authority of the President of the United States, though the President may not actually be present at the moment. It's the same process in deliverance: it may not actually be Michael helping with the deliverance, but he's the one in authority over the warring angels who are sent to deliver. Michael assigns us angels with the authority and power to accomplish whatever it is we have need of.

When we learn to interface with the angels and utilize them effectively, we'll see great power released on behalf of the Lord and His people. To illustrate the point, in 2 Kings 19, one single angel defeats an Assyrian army of over 185,000 soldiers, resulting in the deliverance of Israel from a mighty enemy. By the way, that's not the only time an angel fought for God's people. Those events are historical fact, and they also point out a deeper truth: God has assigned beings of great power to help His people combat an enemy that is stronger than we are by ourselves.

To look at it another way, we are in a great battle. If we fight alone, in our own strength, not one of us will survive. But we've been given weapons of spiritual warfare that are mighty in God. We have spiritual armor that protects and preserves us. We have mighty, vicious angelic warriors fighting alongside us. And over all of it, we have the omnipotent Holy Spirit showing us how to use not only the weapons and companions He has given us, but His very power as well. God has given us all we need and more.

This all leads us to an important truth: we always worked alongside the Holy Spirit and the warring angels to minister deliverance. Never try to minister deliverance apart from both the Holy Spirit and the angels of the Lord working with you! That will not work and it's not likely to end well for you. But as you submit to the Holy Spirit and His leading and learn to call on the warring angels, charging them to do the Lord's will, you're being trained. Eventually, it gets so far down in your spirit man that you don't even have to think about it to do it anymore. The Holy Spirit just brings it out of you as He leads in the moment.

So in short, there is a war going on in the heavenly places. There are full-out battles occurring here on the planet. Things are happening that we have never experienced before. We are about to step into a realm of which nobody has any knowledge. To rely on the Holy Spirit will be the only way we will survive. Furthermore, the Holy Spirit is able to reveal the mighty ministers God has already given us to help us in this war. It is time for us to learn from the Holy Spirit how to live and operate in the supernatural so that we can not only survive what is coming, but thrive in doing so.

And so as we are led by the Spirit, we'll begin to unify and come to one body, one Man. God is working tirelessly, changing our hearts to line up with His plan. When we get all our parts together, we'll become a true army. God has called us to be soldiers, not a bunch of wimps like the body has been in the past. We are warriors who have been given the job and privilege of destroying the works of the devil.

Say Father

CHAPTER 8
UNDERSTANDING DELIVERANCE

Part of the reason so many church-going people who claim to believe the Bible shy away from the area of deliverance is that they're just plain scared of demons. They've not truly believed what the Bible has to say about the authority of the believer and the power of the name of Jesus. They're scared to enter the fray because they think the enemy is stronger than we are. What utter and complete nonsense!

But that kind of thinking is why we have denominations and churches teaching that a believer can't even have a demon. And the result of that kind of teaching is that there are literally thousands of Christians walking around defeated instead of victorious. Let's make it our aim to change that! Greater is He who is in us than he who is in the world.

So let's walk through some of the basics of deliverance and the glory that can be revealed when Christians start to tear down strongholds and boot out the enemy soldiers who have given them such a hard time.

At a basic level, deliverance is allowing the Holy Spirit to reveal what areas of our lives the devil or his agents are ruling over or affecting. When the Holy Spirit shows us something, our job is to listen as He explains what it is and why it is there. Many times, a spirit is operating because, wittingly or unwittingly, we gave it a legal right to do so. Here's a basic rundown of some of the ways we give access to the enemy:

- **Willful sin** – if you're sinning and you aren't interested in stopping, don't be surprised if some demons take up residence and start further influencing you toward sin.
- **Curses** – sometimes Satan's agents can curse us, or the curse may come from those in our lives who simply speak words that

do not line up with God's will for our lives. Words empower either heaven or hell to work in our lives.
- **Iniquity** – sins can be passed down through generations, so many times people will have spirits in operation that came through the family line.
- **Unforgiveness** – Jesus taught us that refusing to forgive others leads to our being turned over to the tormentors – that means we either forgive those who sin against us or we invite demons into our lives.
- **Trauma** – emotional or physical trauma often presents the devil an opportunity to enter our lives. He doesn't care about fairness, and he has no mercy, so he has no problem using those traumatic events in our lives as a point of entry.

Most of the time, the spirits operating in a person's life have gained access through one of these entry points. There are other ways for a spirit to gain entry, however, and I'll discuss some of those later on. For now though, let's say that the Holy Spirit has highlighted some area of our lives where the enemy has access. The very first thing we ought to do at that moment is ask Him to show us why and how those spirits got there. We repent of any sin or iniquity, ask for forgiveness, and forgive those we need to forgive. That by itself can go a long way toward setting someone free! But it gets even better.

Once we have received and given forgiveness, we destroy any curses in operation. And finally, we allow the Lord to heal any trauma we've experienced, both physically and emotionally. What we've basically done at this point is tear down the walls of the enemy's house. He's standing there exposed, just waiting for us to deal with him!

At this point, working with the Holy Spirit and the angels God has assigned to us, we cast those dumb devils out and invite the Holy Spirit to fill up the place where they were. Then we keep our focus firmly on the Lord and His will for our lives, and we commit in our hearts to continue walking in the freedom He has given us.

In a nutshell, deliverance is a powerful ministry of the Holy Spirit as He shows us what is at work, why it's there, and how to kick it out of our lives so He can more fully manifest His glory in and through us. When you think of it like that, who wouldn't want deliverance?

Now, it's important to understand the difference between

deliverance and exorcism. Exorcisms are done by the Catholic Church, they are done by covens of witches, and they're done by the Christian Science church. These kinds of people will claim to cast a demon out of someone, but that's not really what's happening. Exorcism is really an exchange of demonic spirits. It's not a deliverance from them. The demonic spirit level is always increased by exorcism, not decreased.

For example, if a person has severe headaches, they may go to a Christian Scientist. They may pay the man, and he'll pray for them. Now the spirit of headache may leave, but it is replaced by the spirit of brain tumor. They may not have headaches for years, but then all at once the headaches will return. When they go to the doctor, they'll find out they have a brain tumor that's possibly inoperable. That's an example of how exorcism actually works.

Whenever you allow yourself to come under that kind of situation, what you're really coming under is the spirit of witchcraft. Witchcraft is any form of rebellion against God or direct violation of God's will. So these Catholic exorcists or Christian Scientists may even believe they're trying to help, but they're going about it in a way that does not line up with the Word of God. They use rituals or incantations that have no basis whatsoever in the Bible, which equates to participation with witchcraft.

Whether they know it or not, anyone trying to perform an exorcism is basically just opening the door to a higher ranking devil. That's why it seems successful in the moment, but has so much more severe consequences down the road. Of course the low-ranking demons will leave to make room for the higher-ranking ones! And if someone has gone in for an exorcism, they've signed off on the exchange. The enemy doesn't even have to work for it.

So the truth of it is that whenever you allow any person to pray for you who's involved in witchcraft, you're going to get a spirit of witchcraft and divination, and all kinds of demonic spirits will enter you. Only allow those who serve Jesus and only Jesus to deliver you from demons. Otherwise, you're signing up for all kinds of trouble.

Another important issue is that, as I've said, most people in the church as a whole will ask, "How can I have a demon in me, since I'm covered by the blood of Jesus?"

First of all, most pastors don't even really understand a

very basic biblical truth: we are beings who have a spirit, soul, and body. A great many pastors never even teach on this subject. Furthermore, a lot of those who do teach about it start from the wrong place: they describe our existence as body, soul, and spirit. This is not accurate. You are not a physical being who has a soul and spirit. You are a spirit that has a soul and lives in a body. Starting from the right point helps clear up some of the misconceptions.

You see, the bloodline of Jesus is not around your body and soul because those parts of you aren't the "real" you. The spirit man is the "real" you. The blood of Jesus covers your spirit man and protects it against demon possession. Think about it: if the blood of Jesus covered your physical body, you could not get sick, you could not have an injury, and you couldn't have any kind of disease. There could not be any kind of sin in you, period, because the blood of Jesus is sinless.

Therefore, while it is absolutely true that the blood of Jesus has redeemed your spirit beyond the reach of the devil, it is also true that we continue to work out that salvation in our souls and bodies. The goal is to remove all influence of the devil from every part of us. We want our souls and bodies to be just as pure and sinless as our spirit man is. That's why we need deliverance.

The problem the church has is not understanding what they really are. If you don't understand what you are, how can you understand who you really are in Christ Jesus?

I hear people say, "Well, I'm just an old sinner saved by grace." That's a slap in the face to the Lord Jesus Christ and what He did on the cross. It is more accurate to say, "I *was* a sinner, and I *was* saved by grace so that no man can boast, but I am *now* the righteousness of God in Christ Jesus." Now that doesn't mean a Christian never sins, but they don't live in sin. They don't plan to sin or function in sin the way a "sinner" does. You can't be a Christian and a sinner. You are one or the other, not both. The difference between a sinner and a Christian is that the sinner will always sin, and the Christian will occasionally sin. But we have a process of repentance to turn away from sin.

That highlights another essential truth. Many people will ask the Lord for forgiveness, but they do not repent for sin, meaning that they're going to go back and do the same thing again. Carolyn and I have had people come to us for deliverance, but all they wanted us to do was get the "monkey" off their back so they could go back and do what they were doing. So once I figured out what they were trying to do, I stopped them. It's hurtful to them because when they do that, they're opening the door for seven more demons worse than the ones cast out (Matthew 12:43-45). Christians have the opportunity to repent, which keeps that terrible end from happening.

Just as important as repenting of sin and receiving forgiveness, forgiving others has a powerful effect in deliverance. As Jesus taught, whenever a believer does not forgive others, neither will the Father forgive that believer (Matthew 6:15). Furthermore, Matthew 18 shows how the Father will turn over anyone who does not forgive to the torturers, and it doesn't take a genius to figure out what that means.

We've seen so much breakthrough come because people finally forgave people for what they'd done. In order to really forgive, you have to understand a few things. First, forgiving what someone did, does not mean it was right for them to do it. Many times what they did was absolutely horrible! But to continue to carry around things that happened days, months, or years ago is not healthy, and it becomes poison in the spirit. Forgiveness is the antidote that allows us to cleanse that poison from our being.

Second, forgiving others is not optional. We were commanded to do so, which means if we don't, we're choosing to walk in blatant disobedience to God's Word. Finally, forgiveness doesn't have anything to do with whether or not you "feel like doing it." So many people think they just need to wait until they really feel like forgiving. Have you ever noticed that these people often haven't forgiven someone yet? The truth is that forgiving someone is a choice you make. If you wait until your emotions give you permission to forgive, you'll be waiting a long time. We are not supposed to be ruled by emotions, we're supposed to rule over them by obeying the truth. When we choose to forgive, we can expect our emotions to line up with that choice. Don't miss out on the freedom the Lord offers simply because you have chosen not to forgive someone.

Another important part of deliverance is dealing with any kind of traumatic experience. For example, whenever you have any kind of traumatic experience, like a car wreck, or any kind of injury, there is a spirit that enters you at that point called trauma. Trauma is a door opener for every kind of demon spirit of sickness, disease, and sin available at that moment to enter you. They'll enter in and disperse through your entire body.

The way I learned about that was through a phone call I got once from a young man whose fiancé was suffering intense pain. She had been in a car wreck, and since that time, she had suffered such pain that she couldn't stop crying day or night. Even the strongest painkillers did her no good whatsoever. She had even taken morphine, but still the pain was unbearable.

So I called her and began to pray for her for healing. The Holy Spirit stopped me and told me to deliver her instead. When I asked Him what to deliver her from, He showed me in the spirit a comic book of all things! But the comic book showed a man running from a swarm of hornets with one hornet leading and a multitude of hornets following. That leading hornet represented the spirit of trauma, and the rest represented every form of sin, sickness, and disease. I understood that when those spirits enter in through a person through that impact, that traumatic experience, they disperse throughout the person's entire body. Sometimes they feel pain like the young woman did. Other times they'll feel nothing at all, but later on the spirits will manifest through pain or some kind of disease or sickness.

At any rate, when I prayed for this young woman the way the Lord had told me to, she was miraculously healed and delivered.

Practically speaking, when we pray with someone, we always ask them to tell us about trauma they've experienced. We also ask the Holy Spirit to reveal it to us. As we follow the Holy Spirit's lead, we invite him to come and heal the trauma the person suffered. Then we deal with the spirit of trauma. After that we deal with any spirits that entered with trauma, every similar or kindred spirit that operates with or through or is tied to those spirits. When you pray that way, you get five kinds of spirits at one shot! Those little tidbits of information that you pick up increase the power of deliverance and decrease the time involved.

One final element of deliverance that many do not understand is the fragmented soul. Many people are so fragmented in their souls that they cannot even think straight. They're literally not "all there."

At a basic level, the fragmented soul means that parts of people's souls are being "broken off," so to speak, and stolen. This occurs as a result of witchcraft, sexual intercourse outside of marriage, or other ungodly activities. It makes sense when you consider the enemy's job description in John 10:10, which is to "***steal, kill, and destroy***" (emphasis mine). I never understood this until the Holy Spirit instructed me to pray for stolen soul fragments to be returned to someone I was praying with. Since then, I've prayed that countless times, and I've witnessed the change that takes place as people are made whole. The Holy Spirit revealed a vital part of seeing people receive their wholeness, and I now pray that regularly as a part of deliverance sessions.

The Lord confirmed the truth of stolen soul fragments as I dealt with people who wanted to come out of witchcraft and the occult. Former witches have described to me how they stole and took captive fragments of souls, and the real kicker is that it was easy for them because of the ignorance most people live in. That's just another example of why we have to continually allow the Holy Spirit to teach us what we're dealing with and how to effectively pray for people.

The Holy Spirit also showed me that whenever a soul is fragmented or stolen, there can also be fragmented soul parts left in that person from the other people he or she has had ungodly associations with, especially sexual encounters. Not only do the fragments that have been stolen need to be returned, but the soul parts left from others need to be escorted back to the rightful owner.

Let's say you're praying with Sandy, whose soul has been fragmented by ungodly sexual encounters with Billy. First, call upon the warring angels to escort the ministering angels as they return the fragments of Billy's soul left in Sandy back where they belong. Then, command Sandy's soul parts to be returned to her, also escorted by warring angels and ministering angels. Finally, ask the Holy Spirit to restore Sandy's soul and make her whole and complete.

Through this process, the believer has effectively closed off all the points of access that the enemy has gained. From that point, we proceed to cast out the spirits at work by the power of the Holy Spirit and the name of Jesus, and we ask the Holy Spirit to fill people up with His Presence so there's no more room for the enemy to operate.

All of that is a short description of the kind of things that happen in deliverance. This ministry is designed to remove the chains, burdens, and influences of the devil and free up believers to walk into the destiny and purpose God has planned for them.

As I've noted, there are many Christians who simply don't believe that these things happen. But it's the truth. Truth can only make you free if you know it, believe it, and act on it. The Word of God does not say the truth will do anything for someone who doesn't believe it or enact it, let alone someone who's never even heard it before. Once you know the truth, good or bad, then you can deal with it. That's yet another reason why believers must constantly ask and allow the Holy Spirit to lead us into all truth. Otherwise, we're stuck, and I don't know about you, but that's not what I want for myself or those God has placed in my life.

Freedom is much better.

CHAPTER 9
THE PROCESS OF DELIVERANCE

In the last chapter, I gave what I would consider a very brief overview of deliverance ministry and what it can entail. In reality, it can get much more in-depth than what I've described in this book. You have to remember that the Holy Spirit has been teaching Carolyn and me about deliverance for over thirty-seven years and counting. It's not easy to condense all we've learned and done in that time span into something you can read in a matter of hours.

Nevertheless, it is my hope that I can pass on what He's taught us in such a way that empowers all who hear or read it to truly do the work of the Kingdom! So, building on what we discussed in the previous chapter, I'd like to continue forward with a more specific outline of what we generally do when we're praying with people.

Before I do that though, please keep in mind that what I'm presenting you with is not a formula. If you try to turn deliverance ministry into a formula to follow, you're setting yourself up for failure. The minute you lock yourself into a formula, Satan will learn that formula and throw something at you that you've never seen or heard of before. Then you're in a world of trouble.

Everything I'm about to give you comes from the experiences we've had over the time that God has called us into this ministry. It has proven successful time and time again. But the reason this works is that we continue to focus intently on hearing and obeying the Holy Spirit. That is the first and final step here, along with everything in between. The Holy Spirit is stronger, smarter, and much more powerful than the enemy and all of his forces combined, and you won't go wrong as long as you allow Him to lead you as you minister.

So to begin with, I'd like to return to a topic we touched on in the previous chapter, and that is the subject of forgiveness. It's pretty common knowledge that God wants us to forgive the people who sin against us. He even put that in the Lord's Prayer! I'm glad that forgiveness is becoming more and more of a prominent subject in the church.

However, one of the biggest problems I see with many deliverance ministries is that they don't deal effectively with forgiveness. In order to completely minister forgiveness and help someone receive the deliverance they need, you absolutely have to destroy ungodly soul ties. Notice what I said: not all soul ties, just ungodly soul ties. There is a difference.

As we will discuss more in a later chapter, Satan will try to pervert everything God does. The soul tie is just one example of how Satan perverts and pollutes something God intended for good. God works through soul ties – for example between husband and wife, parents and children, or between members of the body of Christ who are led to enter into covenant relationship. These are godly soul ties put in place for God's righteous purposes.

Satan's perversion of the soul ties – the ungodly soul ties – bring division, chaos, and utter destruction. For example, we've dealt with countless individuals who earnestly desire to break free from toxic relationships, but they find themselves returning to the very ones causing them so much pain. They try and try to get away, but they keep going back. Why do you suppose that is?

The reason this happens is because there is an ungodly soul tie at work. That ungodly soul tie results in the control, manipulation, and destruction of the one in whom it is at work. Their emotions seem to have gone haywire, their mind or judgment may be clouded, and they may act in ways that are absolutely contrary to their normal character. When someone is behaving this way, especially in the case of toxic relationships, that is clear evidence of ungodly soul ties at work.

Furthermore, in the case of soul ties, there is a ruling and controlling spirit assigned to the individual to keep manipulating them through the soul tie. That spirit treats the person like a bird on a string: he or she will get so far, just far enough to taste a little bit of freedom, and the spirit will jerk them right back into their state of disarray. The overall assignment of these types of spirits is to maintain a state of un-forgiveness. You may have forgiven another person to the very best of your ability, but that ruling and controlling spirit will bide its time and then slap you in the face with whatever the other person did wrong. Then, without intending to, you find yourself angry or bitter all over again.

So in order to take the process of forgiveness to its fullest effect, have the person you're praying with call the person they're forgiving by name for the specific things they need to forgive. Once that's done, have the person pray, "Father in the name of Jesus, I call upon Michael to take your sword and destroy all ungodly soul ties between (name) and me, and between me and (name). Michael, take your sword and destroy them now, in Jesus' mighty name!" When they've prayed like this, they'll generally sense it in their belly area. Now, as soon as the ungodly soul ties are destroyed, then have them command that the controlling and ruling spirits of the person being forgiven be cast out in Jesus' name: "Father it is my will and I have chosen to forgive (name). Therefore I command the ruling and controlling spirit of (name) to come up and out of me now. I call upon Michael to sack it up, jerk it out, and take it away in Jesus' name." Once all this is done, then the forgiveness is complete.

When people stop short of this full process of forgiveness, trying to forgive can feel like a revolving door because the two things that keep forgiveness from fully happening – ungodly soul ties and ruling, controlling spirits – were never removed. Therefore, the un-forgiveness remains because it keeps getting brought back. But when we remove those things that would keep a believer in un-forgiveness, then we can see forgiveness take its full effect as ungodly soul ties are destroyed and ruling, controlling spirits are cast out.

Once these steps are complete, the person you're praying for also needs to forgive himself or herself. Many Christians don't even realize they have to forgive themselves! But once they do forgive themselves, oftentimes they feel the complete release as the peace of God comes upon them. It is beautiful.

But, as I've said, a great many people, even those ministering in deliverance, do not see the breakthrough they know is available because they're not effectively dealing with something as simple as forgiveness.

And so, many people are not as successful as they want to be in deliverance ministry because they are not effectively dealing with what I call the "preliminaries." The preliminaries include repentance for any willful sin. Next comes the full process of forgiveness as I've just described it. Then, the person you're praying for will also need to forgive his or her forefathers for the sins they've committed because these sins get passed down as generational and inherited curses. The person can repent on behalf of himself or herself and his or her forefathers and receive the forgiveness and cleansing of God. Then, you can release the warring angels to destroy every generational curse passed down from the ancestors and cast out the spirits assigned to those curses in Jesus' mighty name!

Once you've gotten this far, the next step is to deal with all the witchcraft that has been in families for centuries and that goes generations back. This includes destroying curses, hexes, vexes, spells, wishes, incantations, chants, charms, enchantments, all rites and rituals, all words spoken over, about, or against you, all workings, and all generational and inherited curses. Destroy all of these back to their beginnings in Jesus name. Then dispatch the warring angels to capture the words in the atmosphere and all written documents and destroy them back to the beginning. Then you destroy shields, seals, oracles, circles, pyramids, veils and all such protective devices.

All of the things I just named are preliminary. It may take anywhere from fifteen minutes to three hours, but whatever it takes, it is essential to go through these preliminaries. It's basically removing any area where the enemy may hide or claim legal ground. Once you've gone through these preliminary rounds, then you can really get some deliverance.

Proceeding forward, there are certain deliverance issues that are common to every human being. These need to be dealt with early on in the deliverance session. They include hurt, deep hurt, rejection, rejected, rejection in the womb, grief, sorrow, and bitterness.

When you pray with someone over these issues, simply tell them to say "Father," and lead them word for word through a prayer like this: "Father in the name of Jesus, I bind every spirit of hurt, deep hurt, rejection, rejected, rejection in the womb, grief, sorrow and bitterness. I also bind every spirit kindred to these that operates with and through them and every spirit tied to them in Jesus name. Holy Spirit, I ask You in Jesus mighty name to push those spirits up and out of me now. Michael, bind them in the chains of Jesus, sack them up and pull them out of me, in Jesus mighty name!"

You'll often see the authority of the Lord rise up in the person you're praying for as you lead them in this kind of prayer. One issue we've discovered is that there are times where someone has made agreements with or submitted to certain spirits. In those cases, you may have to have the person say, "It is my will, I have chosen, and therefore I command these spirits to leave in Jesus name."

Additionally, nearly every person has the need to deal with spirits of anger, hate, murder, rage, vengeance, violence, vindictiveness and every spirit kindred to them that works with and through them, and every spirit tied to them. Pray in a manner similar to what I included above.

At this point, it is time to ask the Holy Spirit what comes next. Holy Spirit will guide you to the heart of what each person has had to deal with in their lives. We often have no clue what someone's background is, so the way we minister effectively is to get rid of the smaller stuff common to all people, then get to the root cause of whatever has happened in that person's life. You never truly know how to start to minister deeply to someone until the Holy Spirit reveals how to go about it.

Just recently, we ministered to a person and had no clue what all they had been through. On the outside, this person looked so neat and clean, but on the inside – it was just nasty. Another time we dealt with a lady who was an international speaker. She was really pretty; on the outside, her appearance was perfect. When we got into the deliverance, however, we discovered how ugly she was on the inside.

During the deliverance, my middle son, who was praying for her with us, saw the spirit of cancer operating in her. The Lord actually took him inside the woman's head and showed him the cancer cells there. My son is an artist, and he drew what the cells looked like. Recently, a magazine article was written about how they've finally managed to photograph brain cancer cells – they look exactly like what my son drew.

After he saw the cancer in this woman's brain, my son was taken into the woman's abdominal regions, and he saw the cancer there as well. When he saw that, my son jumped up and went running into the garage. Carolyn went out to get him, and he told her he never wanted to see that stuff again! That was actually very unwise of him; the Lord had given him an amazing gift, and if he had continued in it, he could have been a real asset in ministry. Anyway, the point of that example is to show that you cannot gauge what is happening inside someone by your own knowledge or by their appearance. You must rely on the Holy Spirit to guide you.

Something I'm sure you've noticed in the prayers I included is that the Lord told us to utilize Holy Spirit to push demons up. Then we call on Michael to sack demons up and jerk them out.

For example, the prayer goes, "Father, in the name of Jesus, I bind every demon spirit of anger, hate, rage, murder, wrath, vengeance, violence, vindictiveness, and every spirit that is kindred to them with the mighty chains of the Lord Jesus Christ. Holy Spirit, I ask you to push them up. Michael, I call on you to sack them up and jerk them out of me in Jesus mighty name."

Now, the angels who work with Carolyn and me know where they're supposed to take the demons. But the question has been asked many times, "Where are the demons supposed to go?" I asked the Lord long ago, "Lord, where am I supposed to send these things?"

He said, "Where do you want them to go?"

So I said, "Lord I don't want them to come back or to be free to go into someone else, so if I send them into the pit or into hell, Satan will just release them to come back."

He asked me again, "So where do you want them to go?"

I said, "Well how about a nice place in the Sahara Desert?"

"That'll work!"

So we have a place in the Sahara Desert that has millions of demons in it, and the warring angels are holding them there until the Lord Jesus Christ Himself releases them. People tell me they don't believe it, but I don't care whether they do or not. It works, and that's what I'm after.

Many times in ministry, you'll find that the names of spirits come out of your mouth supernaturally. Even the person you're praying with had no idea those spirits were at work, but the Holy Spirit brings them to light, and you get the honor of casting them out. There may also be times where you don't address every single spirit on the lists I've described. You may discover similar spirits with different names or working in different combinations in someone's life. This is meant to keep people off balance, but the Holy Spirit is never fooled. He knows what to do to set someone free. So you keep asking Him to show you what to pray, and when He says, "Stop," you stop. By the time you've done all this, you should expect to see some changes in the people you're praying for.

To review, this basic process is what the Lord has taught us over the years as we've prayed to see people freed from the power of the enemy and sent forth into God's plans and purposes. No two deliverances ever look the same. It reminds me of how Jesus sometimes did the same task in different ways. Why did He lay hands on one person's eyes but make mud to put on another? We may not know until we get to Heaven, but what we do know is that Jesus did it that way because that's how the Holy Spirit led Him to do it.

We have to have that same mentality in deliverance. But when we do, He leads us to victory every time.

Say Father

CHAPTER 10
ALWAYS, ALWAYS DEPEND ON HOLY SPIRIT

When I first started learning about deliverance and walking in the supernatural, my civilian title was engineer, and my military job was Loadmaster for C-97, C-124, and C-130 Air Force cargo airplanes. I was the answer man in everything else I did, but in deliverance, I didn't know "come here" from "sic 'em!" Over the years, I have learned that unless Holy Spirit is directing you in deliverance ministry, you're dead in the water. I've had to learn that following my own understanding and instincts makes the struggle more difficult. Even to this day, I have to fight the tendency to follow my own instinct.

Part of that struggle is because our instincts tell us that there are common elements with every person we deal with, so we may fall into certain habits or patterns as we pray. That may work out fine in some cases. There truly are quite a few common elements with most people. But then you get into the details where those common elements don't exist, and the only way forward is to hear the Holy Spirit.

Early on in our ministry, people began to ask me to come and teach about deliverance ministry. Now remember, this was an area where I did not have extensive knowledge. The first time I taught, I went about this teaching the same way I would if I were giving a presentation to the staff at Tinker Air Force Base. I began with an overview about what I was going to cover, followed by the more specific and technical outlay of that information. At the end, I reviewed what we had covered. I'm sure it was absolutely riveting!

The second time I taught on deliverance was another matter altogether. That time, as I taught, the Holy Spirit took me on what I called "rabbit trails." It just so happened that those rabbit trails covered exactly what the people I was teaching needed to hear specifically for themselves. The Holy Spirit didn't miss a detail.

These days, that's the primary way Carolyn and I teach and minister. We allow the Holy Spirit to give us the rabbit trails that have the answers the specific people we're teaching need for their own personal situations. I never use an outline any more, though sometimes I wish I did. But even though I can be bull-headed at times, Holy Spirit always seems to take over, one way or another. And that's a good thing, because He knows exactly what every person needs. If I relied on my knowledge or instincts, I'd most likely miss those details that can really help set people free.

I'll give you another example of how the Holy Spirit can teach you on the fly. Many people will pray to break the curses operating in someone's life. Now that may seem like a wise thing to do, and it may work for a time. But to break a curse does not actually deal with it in full.

Many years ago, the Holy Spirit spoke to me and said, "My son, that which is broken can be repaired and restored, but that which is destroyed is history." From that time, we no longer pray to break curses, since broken curses can be restored and sent again. We now command those curses and things of that nature to be *destroyed* in Jesus' name. That is a permanent outcome, instead of a temporary one. And we would not have known to pray that way without the teaching of the Holy Spirit.

Furthermore, if you continue in deliverance ministry long enough, you'll eventually find yourself in a situation you haven't dealt with before. Maybe it'll be a situation nobody you know has ever dealt with before. So what are you going to do when that happens?

We may not have the knowledge we need to deal with situations we may find ourselves in, but the Holy Spirit is able to reveal it to us as we have need. Carolyn and I have found ourselves in numerous circumstances, both personally and in praying with others, that we were not prepared for up until that very moment. But the Holy Spirit always quickens us to hear and learn what He needs us to learn in order to overcome. He always leads in triumph if we'll listen and obey what He says.

Sometimes, you learn things you never dreamed of because you experience them for yourself.

Once, in 1995, a professor at Oklahoma University who came to the U.S. from Africa called us asking for prayer. He had been in the country for several years and had a wife and family. He had been suffering intensely from pain in his back, feet, and legs, to the point where he could barely get out of bed. The doctors he had seen could find no problems whatsoever that would cause the pain he experienced. So I invited him to the meeting we were having that night, and I told him he'd be the first one I prayed for.

What we didn't know at the time, but found out later, was that a woman back in Ghana had gone to a medicine man to have a curse put on the professor. She wanted the professor to return to Ghana and marry her.

That evening, when we reached our first break in the meeting, I immediately went to this man and prayed for him. I destroyed the curse and cast the spirits assigned to it out of him. Within a few moments, the professor's pain was gone. But that was not the end of it. Those same spirits I had cast out of the other man now entered me.

It wasn't until later that we found out that there was a curse upon a curse in operation. We had never heard of such a thing! In the meantime, I spent about two weeks in excruciating pain. It would take me about five minutes just to stand up or sit down, the pain was so awful. Carolyn had to roll me around the house on a drafting stool because I could barely walk. Basically, any movement made me feel like I had red hot daggers piercing my back.

Finally, the Lord sent a lady to our house who saw the reason for it all by the Spirit. She saw that over in Ghana, a woman had gone to the medicine man and gotten him to release the curse on the professor. She told us what came upon me was a curse upon a curse, which we had never heard of. But the moment I found out what it was, I was able to destroy that curse and cast the spirits out. Afterwards, I was fine, as though it never happened.

The Lord used that experience to teach us. First, we learned not to merely break curses. What is broken may be reformed, but what is destroyed is destroyed forever. That is an important difference that we, like many others, were unaware of before the Holy Spirit showed us. We also learned to destroy curses upon curses to prevent curses from spreading to those ministering freedom. Holy Spirit is so wise and perfect in the way He teaches us and brings the understanding we need.

Another experience we learned from had to do with Carolyn. She loves praise and worship, and she especially worships through the dance. Because of this, she was targeted by five covens of Indian witches. There was one in Guthrie, one in Wewoka, one in Duncan, one in Anadarko, and one in another location. They were all praying toward us, which formed a star, with Carolyn in the middle. They were attacking her feet, so she couldn't walk. I just about had to carry her around.

While that was going on, a couple who were close friends of ours came over to our house to pray. As we were praying for Carolyn, the wife said, "Ken, I see that there are five covens of witches all praying toward Carolyn!" The Holy Spirit had revealed the witchcraft going on, as well as the cities involved. With that knowledge, we were able to destroy the curses and release the Word of God, and Carolyn was instantaneously healed.

Around that same time, there was also another curse put on her by a Voodoo witch who sat in the balcony at the church we attended. This one was attacking her kidneys. Carolyn was living with constant pain in her back from the kidney area. Once again, the Holy Spirit revealed to us what was going on. We commanded the needle that was being stuck into that voodoo doll to be dissolved in Jesus' name, and we commanded the doll to burst into flames before that witch's face. We did not see whether that happened or not, but Carolyn was healed, and we believe that what we prayed happened. We know what our God is capable of doing!

So we've faced some excruciating pain and difficult times because of things we didn't know about at the time. It all ties back to what the Lord says, "My people are destroyed for lack of knowledge." So once we started learning these kinds of things and how they work, we're able to function more effectively in the Kingdom.

Another time, we were dealing with a young man from down by Duncan, Oklahoma. We prayed for this young man from about one in the afternoon to around nine o' clock at night. He had been a drug addict and alcoholic from the age of fourteen, and he was thirty-eight years old at the time we were praying. He had lived through twenty-four years of addiction. At one point, Carolyn had walked away for a moment, and she returned and said, "Ken, you need to deal with fire water."

Well I already dealt with alcohol, drugs, and everything

else under the sun. Of course at this point in the evening I was tired, and she was worn out too, but she was adamant. "You have to deal with fire water."

So I dealt with the spirit of fire water, and when I did, the young man's neck bulged out like a bullfrog. When that spirit came out of him, it tore his esophagus so badly that one of the women who brought him to us reported he had lain on her couch for three days and nights bleeding from his mouth. But the Lord delivered him from that addiction when we cast out the spirit of "fire water."

Sometimes you think you've got everything down and you know all you need to know, but you may not have everything covered. In this instance, Holy Spirit gave Carolyn the very specific word of "fire water," and that happened to be because the young man was part Indian. Indians talk about "fire water," not "alcohol." That's why I had not seen the breakthrough until the very moment the Holy Spirit gave that specific word.

Another way the Holy Spirit protects us is by keeping us in the truth. When you're dealing with the supernatural, there are so many ways you can get off into deception. As we've discussed before, everything God has ever done, Satan has a perversion of it. Whenever things look really good but something is not quite right, that's probably the perversion.

One way Satan deceives the body of Christ is that he doesn't take us ninety degrees away from the truth. Instead, he takes us just a hair off from the truth. The deception sounds so perfect that people just go with it. They don't discover the deception until the damage has already been done, if they discover it all. When that happens, not only do the ones being deceived go astray, but they also lead others astray with them.

Of course Satan is a liar, but he deceives in such clever ways that very few pick up on most of the deception. He knows he cannot deceive us with blatant lies, but he's clever at drawing us away with things that seem so good. "What a blessing this would be to other people," he suggests, but his intent is to use that little deception to take us right down the drain.

The only way to detect such subtle deception is, once again, to stay focused on the Holy Spirit and the Word of God. He will always alert us when we are straying from the truth. Nevertheless, that does not release us from the absolute need to listen and obey. It's when we feel His correction and ignore it that we are truly in danger.

That is how so many people find themselves caught up in the occult or witchcraft. Much of that filth looks very similar to the power God originally intended mankind to have. However, the source is wrong and the end goal is not the glory of God, but the elevation of oneself, which is the basis of all satanic activity. Remember, Satan fell by trying to raise himself up, and he still deceives people to this day with that same offer: you rise up and take the place of God. It sounds dumb when you read it, but apparently it works.

Continuing on, though, with so much in operation that is not of God, you could never hope to navigate it by yourself. When we line up all the kinds of spirits we're dealing with, there are quite a few kinds. You've got demon spirits, which are also referred to as "unclean spirits" in the Bible. These are disembodied spirits who look for a "home." They're low ranking spirits, but they come in a variety of forms and functions and can wreak havoc if you don't deal with them.

Next, you have fallen angels. These are sometimes referred to as principalities and powers in the Bible because they carry a great deal of authority and power, or rather they did until Jesus disarmed them and took back all authority from them. These spirits often rule territories or people groups because believers haven't come to displace them yet. As Christians, we have to keep in mind that even these high-ranking spirits must bow to the authority of Jesus. Nevertheless, it is essential for believers to combat these fallen angels only by the direction of the Holy Spirit so we don't overstep our authority level.

In addition to demon spirits and fallen angels, there can even be human spirits at work in people or situations. Some people who operate in witchcraft astral project their spirits to wherever they want to go. They use that ability to affect everything from everyday occurrences all the way up to matters of national government. Many believers are ignorant that such a perversion is even a possibility, but it happens.

The first time we ever heard about astral projection, Carolyn was listening to a program on TBN, I believe it was, and on this program was a lady who had been the head witch of England. She was describing how she had astral projected her spirit into the White House, Senate, Congress, and other places, to find out what was going on. That way she had the information she needed to go and do her evil work.

Some people operating in witchcraft even teleport. Astral projection involves sending the spirit, but teleporting moves the whole body. They become invisible when they teleport. They also enter into different animals or birds. I have read books by Kenyan evangelists who used to be sorcerers. They describe how they would transform into flies so they could watch and listen to what was happening in supposedly secure places.

Again, many people simply refuse to believe these things, but that's a choice to operate in ignorance. When you look at the spirit realm, it is essential to research, to ask Holy Spirit to show you what is really happening around you. Ask the Holy Spirit, "What is really going on here? What am I being confronted with in the spirit? What kinds of spirits are assigned to attack me?" The more you learn, the more effective you'll be in dealing with deliverance and people involved in witchcraft.

Let me finish this chapter with this thought: sometimes people get discouraged or intimidated by all the things the enemy can do. That's not why I described it, and that's not the reaction the men and women of God should have. We allow the Holy Spirit to show us these things so that we can effectively combat them.

Never allow the enemy to steal your focus away from the glory and power of God. Always remind yourself that Satan is the head loser and his army has already been defeated in Heaven. The battle rages until Jesus comes back, but there will come a day when we look at Satan and laugh (Isaiah 14:16). God is not in any way intimidated by or worried about the devil, and neither should we be.

The key is to rely completely on the Holy Spirit for everything. If we can get that down, we can rest assured that we will walk in victory over all the schemes of the enemy. The point is not to be impressed with Satan, it is to keep our eyes locked on the One Who can show us how to defeat him and his agents every time.

Say Father

CHAPTER 11
DELIVERANCE TESTIMONIES

I believe that when the body of Jesus Christ begins to truly lay hold of and operate in the ministry of deliverance, we'll begin to see miraculous transformation on a daily basis. In fact, I'll go as far as to say that we really are seeing miracles, healings, and demonstrations of God's glory on a daily basis right now. But I want it to get so ingrained in how Christians operate that we are literally seeing people freed around the clock, twenty-four hours a day, seven days a week.

That being said, I want to share some of the testimonies of what we've seen God do personally throughout our years of ministry. I'm not joking when I tell you that if I were to write them all down, it would fill volumes. I don't say that for you to be impressed with Carolyn and me. Like I said, we were just two people minding our own business and loving Jesus when the Lord called us to this ministry. Furthermore, this is His ministry, not ours. The glory goes to God and God alone for all He has done. All we did was follow Him.

Nevertheless, it is truly amazing what God can do in your life and in the lives of those around you when you learn about and operate in the supernatural power and authority God has given you. Hopelessness disappears before His glory, and even the worst situations can be redeemed. So let me give you a sampling of some stories that show what God has done over the years.

While we were at that same Norvel Hayes conference where we heard the young man speak of being delivered from homosexuality, we had a very interesting encounter. Carolyn and I had met some women from Houston, Texas, and they were staying a few rooms down the hall from us at the same hotel. We decided to go down and chat with them a little. One of the ladies we were visiting told us she had been through deliverance and that she didn't have any demons. When I heard that, I kind of laughed to myself, looked at her and said, "Father, in the name of Jesus, I command the highest ranking demon in her to identify itself by name."

All at once, this lady lunged at me like a tiger! She came bounding at me until she was about six inches from my face, and then it was like she hit a brick wall. Out of her mouth came, "I am Lawanna, and I'm gonna kill her, kill her, kill her!"

I responded by ordering the spirit to tell me what its assignment was, and it revealed that its assignment was cancer. It called itself Lawanna, but its real assignment was to kill this woman with cancer. So we cast that spirit out, and prayed healing for the woman. She became her normal self again. Needless to say, from that point on, she didn't try to claim that she didn't have any demons!

Sometimes the demons operating in a person will stay so subtle and quiet that they never even know those suckers are there. But when the Holy Spirit quickens you to know about them, you'll be ready to deal with them. I can also say with confidence that I have never met a person yet who didn't have some demon or other operating on their life. That's not to glorify the enemy, it's just the truth. Our spirit is under assault all the time, so we have to remain vigilant about it. Furthermore, it's a grave mistake to let pride convince you that you don't have any more work to do to be free. If you're still here and God hasn't taken you to His presence, that's a pretty good sign you have more to deal with. Don't let that discourage you, but do take it to heart and be ready when the fight shows up!

Deliverance can even work on animals. One time, a lady gave us a beautiful little Pomeranian dog. Now this little dog was simply terrified of everything. She was constantly cowering down and acting afraid of the littlest things.

One day Holy Spirit quickened me as I was sitting in my easy chair and the dog was cowering away from me. Holy Spirit told me to cast the spirits of intimidation and intimidated out of her. So I immediately spoke to those demon spirits in that little dog. When I did that, the dog yawned real big and then settled down, and from that day until now she's just the sweetest little fluffy thing you can imagine. I find it encouraging that God cares even for our pets!

Another time we got a call from a group from Denison, Texas, called the Glory Riders. They perform at rodeos and parades and such. They have the most beautiful white horses. One man plays the part of Jesus wearing a white hat and white clothes. Two girls, who play the parts of angels, stand up in the saddle and come streaming into the arena with wings flowing out behind and their white gowns catching the wind of the horses running. All told, it's a beautiful presentation of the Gospel.

When they called us, they told us one of their horses had gotten caught in a barbed wire fence and was cut up really badly. They asked if we'd come down and pray for the horse. I thought, "Well that's unique. I've never done that before."

So I went and anointed that horse with oil and began praying over it and loving on it. I dealt with the spirits of intimidated and intimidation along with the spirit of trauma. That horse yawned like you can't imagine and seemed fine. I thought I was done, but another horse walked right up to me, so I anointed that horse and prayed over it, too. Then another horse, and another began walking right up to me, and before I knew it I was surrounded by about a dozen white horses following me around like little puppy dogs! They all wanted me to pet them and love on them. So I just had a ball with those beautiful horses for a while.

There was another story about a woman with a little weenie dog she left in the bathroom one Sunday morning while she went to church. When she got home, they found the little dog was hanging on one of the little valves under the sink, dead. Her husband started to take it out to bury it, but she said, "Absolutely not!" She brought us that little weenie dog in her purse! She pulled out that little dog and said, "I want you to pray for my dog." So I prayed and commanded life to return into that little dog. All it once it started barking, and its tail was wagging, and it was full of life! We raised a dog to life right there in church.

Then there was another experience with a lady who had brought us into the teaching of the Word. She was extremely sick, and we went to her home late at night, probably around ten o'clock. When we got there, she was deathly sick. When I stepped into the hallway leading to her room, it was like I was swarmed with demons. That place was filled with demons spirits. So we walked back into the bedroom where our friend was and began to minister. As we were praying, she said, "I'm seeing demons everywhere! And I'm seeing skulls and bones. They're everywhere!" All at once, she died. We knew it because we heard that distinctive death rattle.

Once that happened, Carolyn didn't even think twice, she just commanded the woman's spirit to return to her body. Suddenly, the woman started coughing and returned to life. But it wasn't over. A few minutes later, the woman died again. That time Carolyn and I both got into the middle of the fight and raised her up a second time. Then she died a third time and we raised her back up yet again! Each time we heard that death rattle, but each time she came back when we prayed.

Several months later, this same woman came to our home to pray through some deliverance. In the middle of that deliverance session, the spirit of destroyer manifested and started talking to us through her. He told us, "I had her three times and you brought her back!" So this demon confirmed her death wasn't just our imaginations at work – we brought her back from death.

Yet another situation that caught us really off guard was when we were doing deliverance with my son's soccer coach. Now this was back in the early 80s when our knowledge was far more limited than it is now. I like to say, the more you know, the more you realize how little you *really* know about the spirit realm.

Anyway, this soccer coach suddenly went into a coma. We didn't know it was a coma, so we thought she was dead. We shook her and patted her on the face, but she didn't respond. We shouted at her, but still no response. We started wondering what we were going to do. Carolyn even asked if we needed to call 9-1-1, and I was thinking about what we would tell the police.

All at once, Carolyn received the word, "coma." So I addressed the spirit of coma and commanded it to come out of the coach in Jesus' name. The coach started growling at us and sort of came to again. She asked us, "Didn't you hear me scream at you to leave me alone?" I responded that she had never said a word. She told us she had been in a deep, dark, peaceful state and she didn't want to come back. Holy Spirit told me what she experienced was deception unto death, that she would will herself to die because of the deception the enemy had used to trap her.

That's what happens when many people go into a coma,

semi-coma, or deep coma; they literally will themselves to die!

We had another situation where we were dealing with a lady who was born and raised as a white witch. She was responsible for the deaths of at least two people that she knew of, maybe more. We had been dealing with her for quite a while, and it seemed like we'd get so far and then hit a wall. We'd wait a while and work with her more, but we weren't seeing breakthrough.

One evening, we had her over to our house, along with another couple. The other husband is one who sees in the spirit the way most of us watch television. Now, we had prayed a shield of Jesus over our property and covered it with the blood of the Lord Jesus Christ, so no demons could enter from the outside but those who were inside could leave and never return. The angels could come and go.

As we were praying deliverance, all at once, it was as though the young lady's life had left her. The man with the seeing gift told us her spirit was gone! So we commanded her spirit man to return in Jesus name, but the seer told us, "Her spirit is on the outside of the shield. She can't get back in!" So I prayed and caused an opening into the shield which would immediately close so the demons could not come in with it. When her spirit returned to her body, it jerked violently as though a big man had slugged her right in the chest.

I asked her to tell me what happened, and she promised to write me a letter because there were so many things that had just happened. A while after that night, I received a six page letter detailing all that had happened to her during that time.

To summarize, the spirit of Molech had taken her spirit from her body and was dragging her to hell. When I commanded the angels to capture her spirit and bring her back, she had been in a dark tunnel that was becoming colder and colder. Suddenly, she started slowing down, and those spirits taking her down could not push her down anymore because the angels had come to retrieve her. The angels overcame those devils and escorted her spirit to her body. When we prayed for the shield to open, her spirit could finally return. That was a powerful testimony of one snatched from the fire.

And that story brings me to a point that many find uncomfortable: Satan operates in people's lives through the occult and through witchcraft. This is another perversion of God's working.

Just as God operates through the church by way of the Holy Spirit, Satan operates through those he has deceived with a perversion of God's power.

The young woman whose spirit was stolen had subjected herself to the enemy to the point where he was going to literally drag her to hell. Satan will use those in the occult to gain access to people and even territories.

For example, in one April in San Angelo, Texas, Carolyn and I were with a group of people searching out the city to discover and destroy places the enemy had set up so he could control and rule. In one place, the Holy Spirit revealed that there was a vampire spirit living in a tree under a bridge. He'd been there for eons of time. Carolyn could see that it was a very old spirit, wrinkly and gray, and it clawed and scratched trying to stay in that tree. All at once, it had to leave because of the power of the Holy Spirit in us. When it left, it burst into flame and ashes and fell to the ground. Carolyn saw all this in the spirit realm.

But why had the spirit chosen that particular area? Because that area has had lots of witchcraft done in it. Sacrifices had been performed there which enabled that spirit to take up residence and operate for who knows how long!

And don't think this won't happen in your city, too. Young people today are after the supernatural because they're curious about it. They are looking for power. God built into the heart of man a desire for power, so people are going to find some kind of power. Satan is more than happy to share his power with people until he has control of them and takes them over.

That's why we need to learn to help people. We have to learn how to pray to bring people out of the occult and witchcraft. We actually learned some very powerful ways to pray from an experience of praying for two atheists. This way of praying will also work for those you're bringing out of witchcraft and the occult.

This all came about during a meeting we were having in Oklahoma City. Before the meeting, two ladies approached me with a request for prayer. One of them was praying for an uncle in his sixties, and the other was praying for an uncle in his late forties. They had been praying for these uncles' salvation for over twenty years! When I heard that, I asked them, "Well, how have you been praying for them?"

They told me, and I said, "Why are you praying those dumb

prayers?" They looked at me like I'd slapped them in the face. But I explained to them that the Bible says the effective and fervent prayer of a righteous man avails much (James 5:16). The Word doesn't guarantee just saying a prayer will accomplish anything. When we are praying and not getting results, we need to ask the Holy Spirit to teach us how to pray the effective fervent prayers of a righteous man over the situation. How many of us know how to pray correctly over everything? No one does. But the Holy Spirit does, and He can teach us how to pray.

During the meeting, I had everyone pray with us. We began by praying, "Father, in the name of Jesus, we call on Michael, Your chief warring angel, to capture and sever the chords of communication between the controlling and ruling fallen angel that is over these two men and capture and remove those spirits permanently, in Jesus name." After that, we bound the demon spirits that were in the men and commanded that they be bound, gagged, and paralyzed so they could no longer have an influence on these men. Then we dispatched the ministering angels to go to them and start ministering the Word of God in such a way that they could understand and bring people across their paths who could teach them. Next, we prayed for the warring angels to surround and protect them from all evil assignments. Finally, we asked the Holy Spirit to go to them and draw them with such love, conviction, and power that they could no longer refuse the Lord Jesus Christ.

Now mind you, both of these men had been prayed over for twenty years. But within two weeks, both of them were bornagain, Spirit-filled, tongue-talking Christians!

So this shows the difference between a shotgun-style prayer and a rifle prayer. With a shotgun, you're throwing up a lot of lead and hoping you hit something, but with a rifle, you're carefully taking aim and sending a single round straight into the target. When we got straight to the heart of the issue, we saw the Lord move. So we need to learn to pray over these situations that are so destructive to humanity. We have to be led by the Holy Spirit in order to accomplish the kind of work that the Lord wants out of each situation.

I want to add to all this that deliverance is not just for adults. Children are under attack as well, and they can also receive great freedom through deliverance.

Many people have a problem with taking children through

deliverance. But children don't have a problem with it – they already know about demons! Carolyn has learned how to talk to even little children in deliverance. She'll give the child a piece of printer paper and a crayon or a pen. Then she'll start asking the child questions, and they'll draw out what their problems are. Carolyn will ask, "What is this you've drawn?" These little children will literally tell you where the demons are and what they are.

Once we dealt with a little five year old girl who was a witch. She could speak to the wind and it would stop. As we were working with her, Carolyn took her in and did with her what she does with other children. This little girl started drawing out what looked like an eagle. She called it the spirit of "Eagl-ey." Carolyn asked, "Where did this spirit come from?" The girl said it had come on the wing of an airplane and drew out the airplane. To make a long story short, we delivered this girl of a whole bunch of stuff. Two or three weeks later, we saw her at church. She came up and told Carolyn that "Eagl-ey" was still over in the Sahara Desert, where we sent that spirit during deliverance.

Dealing with children like this is a little different, but it can be effective if you use the process of having them draw out what's going on. It's best to send them with one person away from the other adults so they'll feel more comfortable, perhaps into the kitchen or the next room. The kids feel really comfortable with Carolyn, and she can usually take the kids through the drawings and the deliverance process very quickly and easily.

Every one of these testimonies shows how God can move through the ministry of deliverance. If believers in Jesus will press into this type of ministry, follow the Holy Spirit, and allow the Lord to teach them how to operate effectively, we'll see more and more of God's miraculous work on the earth. It's just one more way that we tear down the enemy's kingdom and replace it with the eternal, unshakeable Kingdom of Jesus Christ.

CHAPTER 12
PROTECT YOURSELF FROM THE ENEMY

I want you to understand that just as deliverance ministry applies to the way you help other people get free from the enemy's influence, it also applies to the way you get free and stay free from the schemes and plans of the devil. It is entirely possible to live a lifestyle of ongoing deliverance and freedom by the grace of God.

One of the enemy's greatest tricks is to pretend that he simply doesn't exist. He has convinced so many people that you can just ignore him and he'll go away. The irony of that deception is that it basically gives him a free pass to wreak havoc in people's lives. So the question for you to answer is, do you want to allow any area of your life to come under the influence of the devil, or do you want to remain as free as you can be? I assume, if you've read this much of the book, that you choose the second option, which is the correct choice.

So what I want to accomplish in this chapter is to show you how to apply the principles of deliverance to your own life. That way, you can embrace a lifestyle that tears down what Satan has built and raises up the Kingdom of God.

Living this lifestyle begins with your willingness to value forgiveness. Forgiveness is such a treasure, both for ourselves and for anyone we choose to forgive. When we receive forgiveness for ourselves, it is as though God has erased the effect of sin (Psalm 103:11-14). Furthermore, when we extend forgiveness to others, we offer God the opportunity to heal our wounded souls and bless those who wounded us. It's a double blessing.

And we must always remember that both of these types of forgiveness are available through the sacrifice of the cross. Jesus paid a price that we can barely comprehend. Yet, at the same time, it is such a simple expression of love that God would send His very own Son to the cross so that He could offer sinners forgiveness. That ought to show every person the power of forgiveness. If God thought it was worth the life and death of His Son, how much more should we make forgiveness a central part of our lives?

All this to say, step one in living a lifestyle of freedom is to consistently and persistently forgive those who have sinned against you. Forgive them from your heart. Say, "Father, in Jesus name, I choose to forgive (name them specifically) for (name it specifically). It is my will, and I choose to forgive (name) in Jesus mighty name. Father, I also ask you to forgive (name) for (whatever it was), and to bless them with your best blessing, in the name of Jesus."

When you pray this way, you are making the deliberate choice to participate not in the wounding that the enemy intended, but in the blessing of forgiveness that God has so highly valued. It is also important to remember what we discussed in earlier chapters about completing the power of forgiveness.

Be sure to dispatch the warring angels assigned to you to destroy every ungodly soul tie formed between you and the person you're forgiving. Ask the Holy Spirit to push up and out of you every ruling and controlling spirit of that person. Charge Michael to capture the ruling and controlling spirit and remove it permanently. Next, charge the ministering angels to return any soul fragments to where they rightfully belong. Lastly, ask the Holy Spirit to make both you and the other person completely whole. This way, you're ministering both to the other person and to yourself, and you can expect God's healing to manifest.

Another serious part of this lifestyle of deliverance is to be aware of any trauma you experience, either physical or emotional. Remember that trauma is an open doorway for all kinds of spirits to enter. It is essential that you consistently allow the Holy Spirit to reveal any trauma at work, ask Him to heal you of that trauma, and remove the spirits involved.

Say, "Father, in Jesus name, I bind every spirit of trauma, traumatized, traumatizer, along with every kindred spirit that works in or through them or that is tied to them. Holy Spirit, push them up and out of me now, in Jesus name. Michael, I call on you to capture them, bind them in the chains of Jesus, sack them up and jerk them out of me now, in Jesus mighty name!"

Why would anyone give the devil an open invitation to wreak havoc in their lives? And yet, that's what you do any time you don't deal effectively with the trauma you experience. Living in this world, it is pretty much guaranteed that you'll encounter some kind of trauma, but that doesn't mean it has to turn into such destruction the way it does in so many people. Stay aware of it and deal with it any time you encounter it.

Along with all we've talked about so far, you must also constantly repent for any participation with sin. Repentance must come from your heart, and it must be a serious commitment to turn away from the sin or agreements you've made with the enemy. Without true repentance, you will not receive the freedom you need.

We once dealt with a young lady in Atlanta, Georgia, who had a disease called dystonia. We'd never heard of that before, but she could be walking along as normal as anybody and her body would suddenly start going into extremely painful distortions. So we were asked to go and minister to her.

When we began working with her, she was very thin. She wore a dress with a very tight bodice. As we ministered, all at once, the demons in her manifested, and it literally looked like someone was punching her bodice from inside it, moving it as much as two to three inches. But as we continued to minster, we found out that the disease dystonia is rooted in sexual perversion. This young woman was in the habit of searching out the filthiest, grimiest old truck drivers and taking them to bed. Consequently, the spirits carrying the disease of dystonia entered her. We never did get that spirit out of her because she was unwilling to give up what she was doing. It was a sad case.

However, we did find out from that experience that many times the demons have an assigned date to kill the person they've entered. As we queried the demons in that young lady, they revealed that her assigned date of destruction was September 16, 1989, if I recall correctly. I commanded the demon to tell me how it would kill her, and it told us it would cause her to overdose on her medications.

Again, you find out a lot by querying demon spirits. Some people object, "But won't they just lie to you?" But we have the Spirit of Truth operating in, through, and with us, and He will quicken us to know when the demons are not telling the truth.

Plus, we can call on the warring angels to slap the demons upside the heads with their swords and make them tell us the truth. There are things going on in the spirit realm that we can't see or do in the physical, but we can call on the warring angels to do them in the spirit, and things start happening quickly.

Nevertheless, in this particular case, we could not break this woman free because she was not willing to repent. Let that be a warning to you as well.

Stepping into another area, we need to realize that, since it is under the control of Satan, the world system wants us dead. To illustrate, if you go to the Stonehenge of Georgia, or the Georgia Guidestones, you'll see written in eight languages instructions for the world population to be reduced below 500 million. Currently, the world population is over seven billion. The question is how the powers that wrote those instructions intend to accomplish that task. Machine guns or bombs would bring complete disaster. Instead, they'll use four primary things: 1. things released into the air, 2. things put into water, 3. things they're putting into food, and 4. things they put in medications.

So we need to learn how to neutralize whatever enters our body that is not of the Lord. We have authority to cause poisons and chemicals to absolutely neutralize and be non-effective in our bodies. We do it by the words of our mouths: "Father, in the name of Jesus, I command all poisons and all chemicals in my body to be neutralized and to pass immediately from me, in Jesus' mighty name."

The Bible promises that those who believe in Jesus can eat or drink deadly poisons without being affected. We need to believe that and act on it if we're going to see it manifest!

In a similar sense, every believer needs to be aware of word curses operating in and on his or her life. Unfortunately, there are more word curses put on the body of Christ by other Christians than there are by witches. How can that be? It's because a whole lot of people let their alligator mouth overload their hummingbird legs. They say things they shouldn't say, and they put curses in place, simply because of jealousy or some other meaningless trifle that's not even worth opening their mouths about. Nevertheless, those words give demon spirits a right to attack the person they're speaking about, whether they meant for that to happen or not.

So a lot of people need to learn to simply keep their mouths shut. If there's something you don't like, simply walk away from it without cursing it! Don't let your words provide an opportunity for the enemy to operate in someone's life.

It's a sad truth that a lot of people put word curses on themselves, also. The Lord actually corrected me quite firmly for the curses I spoke over myself. Flying people have a tendency to use the expression "crash and burn" when they get so tired they can barely function. Back in 1981, Carolyn and I had gone to a Kenneth Copeland conference, and we were walking up the stairs headed back to the hotel room. I made the statement that I was going to "go crash and burn," just because I was so wiped out.

Holy Spirit spoke through a lady and said, "My son, you shall never speak those words again because you are creating your own demise." From that time on, I've never used that terminology again. That's just one example of how people can speak the worst curses over themselves. So what you have to do is be aware of the words you use, especially about yourself. Satan doesn't care if you're just kidding. You have to remain vigilant, choose to speak blessing, and allow the Holy Spirit to show you anything you've spoken that is not His will. Be very quick to repent and destroy ungodly words.

Continuing on, as you're walking in freedom, you'll need to deal with spirits that have transferred to you from the people or places you've encountered. One of the sneakiest things the demons will do is transfer from other people or the places we go. Again, a lot of people think that because they're Christians, spirits cannot transfer to them, but that's simply not the case.

The key is to learn to deal with the spirits that have transferred to you. A prayer my wife and I pray almost every day is, "Father in the name of Jesus I command every demon spirit that has transferred from another person to me today to be bound with the chains of Jesus. Holy Spirit I ask you to push them up. Michael, sack them all up and jerk them out of me in Jesus mighty name."

And you find that wherever you go, whether it's to a shopping mall or a church or wherever, you're going to run into people who have demons, and those demons are going to try to transfer from them to you. How do they do that? I'm not exactly sure, but I know they do. It's wise to be aware of this sneak attack and learn how to deal with it.

The point to understand is that we've not reached perfection yet. We've met people who've *thought* they'd reached perfection, but of course they're still here with us, so we know that wasn't the case. Since we've not reached perfection, there are still places for demons to transfer to us from the people we meet and places we go. It's not something to be afraid of, but it's something to be aware of and keep your temple cleaned out on a regular basis.

Carolyn and I went to church at a place in Norman, Oklahoma, years ago, and we took a young man with us. During the church service, the young man said, "I keep hearing a voice telling me, 'You're home, you're home.'" We didn't think much of it at the moment, but a week or two later we went to that church again, this time with a lady we knew. She heard a voice telling her the exact same thing, so now we had our antennas up, so to speak.

A few months later, we were doing deliverance in our home with two women from northern Oklahoma. On top of that, while the deliverance was going on with the two women, we got a phone call. Carolyn answered and began doing deliverance with the person on the phone. We had three deliverances going on all at the same time!

One of the spirits in the women I was praying with started speaking out. I commanded it to tell me what was the business of the voice saying, "You're home, you're home" in Norman, Oklahoma. It started laughing and said, "Don't you know? It's from the greeter." The spirit at work in the greeter was transferring into every person who stepped into that church. The Holy Spirit told us that church was built on sinking sand. There was not much good coming from it, and the goal of that transferring spirit was to deceive people into becoming part of a church that wasn't founded solidly on the word of God. It seemed like a welcome, but it was actually an invitation to deception.

This story illustrates how important it is for believers to remove those transferring spirits on a daily basis.

That leads to another important part of freedom, which is testing spirits. If you're going to hear the supernatural realm, you need to be sure you're hearing from the right source.

On the subject of testing spirits, most people are taught 1 John 4:1-2: "*Beloved, do not believe every spirit, but test the spirits, whether they are of God; because many false prophets have gone out into the world. By this you know the Spirit of God: Every spirit that confesses that Jesus Christ has come in the flesh is of God.*" What they don't realize is that this passage refers to testing the spirit of the prophets, not testing a spirit to determine whether or not it is from the Lord.

The Holy Spirit spoke to me about how to test a spirit. "My son," He said, "in order to test a spirit, whether it is of Me or whether it is a demon spirit, repeat what it said to you, then address the spirit who said it to you. I command you to tell me, 'Do you call Jesus Christ Lord and do you worship and serve Him only?' Answer me now in Jesus' name." A spirit sent from God will testify that Jesus is its Lord and that it serves only Him. If it is not from Him, you may get a sick feeling or hear a screaming "No!" Or you may hear nothing at all. That tells you what kind of spirit is talking to you, so you deal with it quickly and move on.

Remember though, when testing spirits, employ a command, not a request. The Lord told me once, "My son, prayer consists primarily of commands and demands on the spirit realm." Yet, we whine and cry and beg God. That's the wrong thing to do. We are the ones God gave dominion here on this planet, and it's up to us to hook it up and do what's right. In other words, we use the authority God has already given us in our prayers. Instead of crying and begging, we follow as the Holy Spirit leads and command His will to take place on Earth as it is in Heaven.

Many times, Christians simply don't *feel* that we're authorized to pray that way. The reason that happens is because Satan attacks us with spirits of intimidation whose job it is to put us down and make us feel guilty. These spirits try to make us believe we're doing something wrong, but it's not wrong to pray the way God commanded us to pray. Just like Jesus said, we've got to take care of the Father's business! As we learn to effectively deal with the things of the spirit realm, we'll begin to see some different results from the ones we've seen in the past.

For example, one evening we had in our home a young lady to whom we were ministering, and she told us, "A voice told me that if I return to Tulsa, I'll receive my healing."

When I heard that, my spirit was disturbed. So I told her, "You speak to the spirit who just told you that. Say, 'I command the spirit who told me to return to Tulsa to tell me, do you call Jesus Lord and do you worship and serve Him only? Answer me now in the name of Jesus.' Say those words exactly."

Now when she did that, the spirit that had been talking to

her immediately started cussing her out, which of course indicates it had come from the devil. When you command the spirits that way and hear nothing but silence, that also indicates a spirit from the devil. When it is the Holy Spirit or one sent by Him, you'll hear a polite and firm "yes" in response to the question. Oftentimes you'll even get more detail about what the spirit previously said. So it's important to keep these things in mind in order to test the spirits.

One last thing to keep in mind is that we often deal with spirits that are territorial in nature. That means it will require a certain level of spiritual authority to deal with those spirits, and not everyone ought to try. Have I mentioned that it's essential to be led by the Holy Spirit and only do what He says?

Those people who get a little big for their britches and try to tear down a spirit without the leading of the Holy Spirit tend to get whipped. Unfortunately, most people have not been taught that you ought not try to pull down a stronghold that is beyond your level of authority. We've dealt with several people who have overstepped their authority level.

As an example, we met a woman in an IBM meeting a few years ago who was experiencing some intense issues and needed to get freedom. Now, we found out through the deliverance that this lady had stepped onto a mosque property somewhere in Ft. Worth, Texas. When she did that, apparently a spirit of Islam entered her. So as we were casting it out, we commanded the spirit to tell us how it got a legal right to enter. It told us that it could enter in because she stepped onto the property, and its assignment was to kill her.

The spirit got real talkative as I continued to interrogate it. I played dumb and kept asking it questions and letting it talk and tell me different things as it tried to glorify itself. At one point, the spirit boasted, "We're going to bomb everything!"

I said, "What do you mean, 'bomb everything?'"

"We're going to blow this place up. We have suitcase bombs planted all over America."

Now it thought we would be intimidated, but we cast that devil out and saw the woman set freed. But from that time, one thing we've started doing is commanding the trigger devices for those bombs to be neutralized and rendered non-functional in Jesus name. This is just another example of how much you can find out and be effective for good.

But it also shows why, if you're not authorized to pull down a stronghold, you shouldn't do it. As you go to the higher levels of spiritual warfare, you may find yourself dealing with something that only someone who carries the office of a teacher can pull down. The next level up would be someone in the office of pastor, then the office of evangelist. Going even higher, there may be strongholds that only a prophet can pull down. The highest level requires the authority of the apostle to pull it down.

So if you're trying to pull down a spirit that's higher than your level of authority, you'll find yourself in trouble really fast.

Through the years, through the revelations the Lord has given us, Carolyn and I have managed to live a lifestyle that is generally free from the influence of the enemy. We've still found ourselves in battles here and there, but that's to be expected, and we know the Holy Spirit never loses. What I want for you and for every believer in Jesus is to go through life with eyes wide open, not in any way deceived by the enemy nor terrified by him because you're equipped and ready to deal with whatever he throws at you. Living the way I've described in this chapter will give you a great start.

Say Father

CHAPTER 13
CLEANSE THE HOUSE

In addition to keeping yourself pure from the influences of the enemy, it's also essential for you to protect your property, especially your home. God's will is for His people to live in safe, peaceful homes. Isaiah 32:18 says, *"My people will dwell in a peaceful habitation, in secure dwellings, and in quiet resting places."* That makes it clear that chaos is not welcome in the homes of the people of God.

Therefore, you need to constantly deal with driving demons out of your home, especially when a salesman or some unusual person has come into your home. They may have brought spirits with them inadvertently, or they may have purposefully released spirits into your house. So you need to call on the warring angels to capture and remove all demon spirits from your home, the closets, rooms, inner walls, attics, basements, under the floors – basically to clean out the entire home. Then you need to charge those warring angels to stand guard over your home and protect it.

You can also invite the ministering angels to come and take up residence in your home. Ask them to minister to every person who comes in. That takes you out of the defensive posture and puts you on the offensive. Why just defend your territory when you can also release the blessing of God to all who come in?

Also, you need to call warring angels to stand guard over your entire property. To finish it all off pray a shield of Jesus and a canopy over your home. If you read Psalm 91, it describes the complete peace and safety God desires for His people. One verse describes how *"His truth shall be your shield and buckler."* So Holy Spirit revealed to us that we can pray a shield of Jesus as protection around ourselves and our property. In the spirit, the shield literally looks like a sphere, and we coat that shield with the precious blood of Jesus. If you study the Scriptures about what is done with blood, you'll find that it is always sprinkled or applied in some way. So we apply the precious blood of our Savior to the shield, and demons cannot come through that shield! These are the kinds of things you should do as regularly as you clean your bathroom, or more! You just don't want the devil to have any place to operate in your house.

Many times, people will be having problems in their houses, and they don't understand why these certain issues are happening. If you're having problems in your house, ask the Holy Spirit, "What is in my home that has given demons the legal right to be here?" Generally speaking there will be something in the home that is demonic.

For example, from 1961 to 1980, I was bringing items into our home from all over the world. I brought a carving of home from La Paz, Bolivia. This particular carving was made of wood, and it depicted the sun god of Tiahuanaco. I got it because it was unique and different-looking, and I thought it was cool. That was in 1978, before I got saved.

Well, after we got saved, Carolyn was constantly sleepy. All day long, she felt so sleepy she could barely keep her eyes open. She asked the Holy Spirit why she was constantly feeling so sleepy, and He told her it was because of the spirits in that wood carving. So I took that wood carving and numerous other items (which amounted to several thousand dollars in worth), destroyed them, and threw them away. Once we got rid of those items and called on the warring angels to remove those spirits, Carolyn never had another problem with being sleepy.

It's also important to realize that you never want to just give those kinds of things away because you're basically giving demons to someone else. The better option is to destroy them. I prefer to destroy objects in fire so that they cannot be reformed. If that's not possible, cut it up with scissors or a saw, or break it into pieces. At the very least, wrap whatever you're getting rid of in some garbage sacks and toss it in the dumpster.

The point is that you don't want to give objects you know to be demonic to someone else. That just passes the problem to the next person. Instead, do your best to destroy the object and get it somewhere that other people won't be able to find it. That's what we've done in our home, and we've seen breakthrough because of it.

We've also seen similar results with other people. A lady once asked us about the book, *The Lord of the Rings*. She also had a Ouija board in the home. Carolyn went to this lady's home and told her she needed to burn the books and the Ouija board. As the woman burned the items in the fireplace, Carolyn took pictures, and you can literally see the demons in the pictures. Since that time, we've taken many pictures of things being burned and you can often see the demons in them.

We had another call from a man who had found a sex manual in a home he was remodeling, along with a Hindu bible. We put those things in his fireplace to burn them, but they wouldn't light. Finally, I called on Michael to capture and remove permanently the spirits that were protecting those books from burning. At last, we got them to start burning, and that's when it really got fun. We had them kind of standing up and folded out so they'd burn faster, and out of the base of the Hindu bible, a flame shot straight out toward me, made a full 180-degree turn, and shot back in. It hissed the whole time that was happening. Fire does not do that naturally, so obviously the demons attached to that book did not like that we were destroying it.

Another time, we helped a lady who was trying to remove a poster of Freddy Krueger from her kid's bedroom. The demon tied to that poster was resisting her tremendously. She would step in the door and the spirit in that poster would knock her back out into the hallway.

She called me, and I told her to keep the phone to her ear while she walked in the next time. As she went back in, I bound that spirit so it could not resist her, and she got the poster down from the wall. She took it out into the front yard and tried to set it on fire. It took a long time for it to catch, but she finally got it started. However, when she went out the next morning, that poster was still burning. We're talking about a regular poster, which would normally take only minutes to destroy. There was obviously a spirit at work.

We've got all kinds of stories about objects that carried demons, but the point is that the spirits that are doing these kinds of things have a power that most people don't understand. Usually, you won't see that power being used until the demons are confronted by a Christian. Until they're confronted by a believer, the demons don't even have to use that power because they have everything under control. When a believer begins to take dominion, the fight is on. Not to worry, though, because we're on the winning side.

It gets really personal when these kinds of things are going on in your own home, though, and Christians need to know how to drive those demons out. We are the ones in authority, not those dumb devils. So we constantly drive out those things that don't belong, including removing objects the Holy Spirit tells you to remove. That way you're not giving any legal ground for the enemy to operate, and you constantly allow the angels and the Holy Spirit to clean out what doesn't belong.

So let's bring this down to the practical steps to take. First, stay aware of what's going on in your house. Is there a family member behaving differently? Are your objects being moved or broken? Are you or anyone in your house experiencing something out of the ordinary? If so, it's time to ask the Holy Spirit to reveal what is going on.

As you are listening to the Holy Spirit search the physical premises of your house. Allow the Holy Spirit to highlight any object that needs to be destroyed. If he shows you anything or quickens your spirit about it, destroy it immediately in the best and fastest way possible.

Once you've done that say, "Father, in the name of Jesus, I charge the warring angels assigned to me to capture and remove all demon spirits from my home. Remove them from the closets, rooms, inner walls, attics, basements, under the floors, and from every place where they have trespassed. I charge the warring angels to stand guard over my home and to protect it from all intrusion. Now, Father, I charge the ministering angels to take up residence in my home and to minister to every person who comes in here. I release your Word, Father, according to Isaiah 32:18, that my home is a peaceful habitation, a secure dwelling, and a quiet place of rest. I thank you for it, in Jesus mighty name."

Your home is the environment in which you'll spend the most time. It only makes sense to keep that environment as clean as possible, both physically and spiritually. You have the dominion in your house, so whatever you tolerate will remain. Likewise, whatever you bind and forbid must leave. Commit in your heart to keep your home as clean and pure as you can.

Say Father

CHAPTER 14
YOUR SPIRIT-LED PRAYER MAKES AN IMPACT

One truth I really want to get across in this book is that everything that happens in this physical world is the direct result of what is happening in the spirit world. Many people try to separate these two worlds, but you just can't do that. What we see and hear in this physical realm is a reflection of the spiritual world, not the other way around. So if we want to be more effective in any given area of our lives, we have to become more effective at operating in the supernatural.

I really believe that if people could physically see the effect our prayers have, we'd never stop praying. Something is always happening when we pray, whether it is deliverance prayer, prayer over specific situations, or just the communion we share with Father, Son, and Holy Spirit. Every kind of prayer has its own purpose and power, but the point is that we need to be praying constantly. And as I said before, we need to ask the Holy Spirit to teach us to pray the effective, fervent prayers of a righteous man over every situation.

So why don't we do that? I believe it has to do with the discouragement and distraction that Satan throws in our faces to keep us blind to what is really happening. We get focused on what we see, rather than what we know to be true, and when we don't physically see the results of our prayers, it's easy to become discouraged.

That's why I want you to really lay hold of the truth that God always moves when we pray, especially when we allow the Holy Spirit to pray through us. We pray according to His will and He responds. End of discussion.

In this chapter, I want to share some more testimonies of

what God has done in response to prayer in the hopes that you will take courage and keep on praying. Your Spirit-led prayers are powerful, and the worst thing you can do is stop praying.

I want to start with some stories about what God did when He allowed me into the trucking business for a few years. One man who worked for me was named Robert. He was born in New Jersey, just a few miles south of New York City. Now this man was rough around the edges and all the way through. He was the kind of guy that if you ever crossed him, he'd deck you first and ask questions later.

Through the time he spent working for me, I got to know Robert a little bit and found out some interesting details about his life. When he was only eighteen years old, Robert and his dad had gotten into an argument, so Robert went out in the yard and called him out. He kept yelling at his dad to come out in the yard so he could whip the dog out of him (I'm sure he used worse language). His dad never did come out, which I think was wise. I also found out Robert had pulled a knife on another driver once over some dispute or another. Basically, he was a rough and tough guy you didn't want to mess with.

But the Lord put it on my heart to just begin really loving on Robert. I'd treat him with respect and tell him what a good job he did for me as a driver and so forth. The Lord began to soften his rock-hard heart and worked on it. Eventually, I got to lead Robert to the Lord, and that happened only six months before he passed away from cancer.

There was another driver working for me named Jimmy. Jimmy was living with a woman he wasn't married to, and he basically had a terrible life, full of hardships. So I started loving on Jimmy the same way I had with Robert, being respectful and telling him how much I appreciated him and the job he did for me as a driver. The Lord worked on Jimmy's heart like He had Robert's, and after a while Jimmy got saved, too. All of this was the Holy Spirit working through simple acts of kindness and obedience.

Sometimes, though, you have to confront people and allow the Lord to start dealing with their hearts. There was another driver named Wes who worked for a friend of mine. Wes was driving from Denison, Texas, out to California. When he left, he was not feeling very well, and when he got to California, he threw up all over the inside of his truck and started to go blind.

When he called in, one of the men at the office happened to know exactly where Wes was in California and told him there was a truck stop a few miles ahead. If he could make it there, they'd call an ambulance to come pick him up. So Wes made it to the truck stop and the ambulance came and got him and took him to the hospital. When he arrived, he was mere moments from going into a diabetic coma.

After he got straightened out, when he made it back to Denison, I saw him in the office about a week and a half later. I said, "Wes, you need to get rid of that diabetes."

"What do you mean?" he asked.

I told him that diabetes was actually a demon spirit. Well he got real mad, jumped up and went running out of the office. In about two more weeks, he came back into the office again, and I asked, "Wes, are you ready to get rid of that diabetes?"

He said, "I guess you're going to talk about those demons again."

I said, "Well, that's the bottom line of it. If you want to keep them, that's fine by me because they're not eating on me."

He jumped up and stormed out of the office again. About twenty minutes later, his boss came in and said, "Ken, Wes is out in the yard and he wants you to come pray for him."

I walked out into the yard and saw Wes standing there waiting. I walked up and stopped about three feet away, crossed my arms across my chest, and said, "Wes, if you're truly serious, I'll pray with you. But if you're not serious, don't waste my time or yours."

"I'll pray with you," he said.

So I led him through a prayer of deliverance. All at once, he started going, "Whoo! Whoo! Whoo!" Down he went. I mean, he went down to the gravel, and it took a couple guys to catch him before he hit the ground. I was still standing there with my arms crossed and never laid a hand on him. Those other guys got him stood back up and in a couple minutes we had him leveled off, and we finished praying.

Then I said, "Wes, are you ready to receive healing?"

He got really excited then and said, "Yeah!"

I led him through a healing prayer and he prayed with me. Shortly, Wes started going, "Whoo, whoo, whoo" again, and down he went. God supernaturally healed him, and I never laid a hand on him. Afterward, he asked me, "Does this mean I'm supposed to quit taking my insulin?"

"No," I told him. "God has healed you. Do whatever the doctor tells you to do. It's not going to make any difference now."

A few days later, Wes went back to his doctor. The doctor told him, "I don't understand what happened, but you don't have diabetes." To be safe, the doctor told him to keep taking his medicine for the time being. After a while, Wes returned and still had no signs of diabetes. The doctor allowed him to reduce his medicine. Eventually, the doctor completely released Wes from taking any medicine for diabetes. He was completely healed.

These stories, and Wes's story in particular, illustrate the power of the words we speak. In essence, our words penetrate to the spiritual root of any given problem, and they have the power to manifest in the physical world.

Another story that shows how the spirit influences the natural occurred at a church one evening. It was getting late, but after the meeting, a couple wanted to visit with Carolyn and me, so we stayed to visit. Suddenly, the other lady looked over to the side, and her cousin had walked in and sat down. At that point in the night, it was only us in the building.

The lady from the other couple walked over to where her cousin was, then came back and asked us to go pray for him because he was drunk and spaced out on drugs. As we walked over to where the man was, his eyes narrowed and he looked at me and said, "I know you. I know you."

Carolyn said to him, "If you know him, you know me, too."

"No," he said, "I don't know who you are."

As this exchange was happening, the Lord told us to lead him through the sinner's prayer, even though he was drunker than a skunk. So I led him through the sinner's prayer. When I did, the Lord told Carolyn to lead him through the baptism of the Holy Spirit. She said, "Lord, you've got to be kidding!" But the Lord said again, "Lead him through the baptism of the Holy Spirit."

Carolyn led him through the prayers to receive the baptism of the Holy Spirit, and she laid her hands on him. When she did that, he was slain in the spirit and fell to the floor. When he came back up, he was sober as a judge and speaking in tongues.

We learned from that experience that it's not the alcohol or drugs that spaces someone out, it's the spirit of it. You can put that down as a "take-it-to-the-bank" piece of information, along with every sickness and disease. It's a spirit that causes such manifestations, not just something that happens to people because of illness or substances.

Another time a guy in Dallas had contacted us asking for prayer for his friend. She had been to Jamaica, but when she got back home, she became very sick and eventually went to the hospital. Her skin had turned a yellowish green color, and she was in real bad shape. Then, all at once, brown splotches developed all over her body. Her organs began shutting down until all that was functioning was her heart and lungs.

I told the man who had called us and his wife to go up to the hospital. This was probably around ten at night, and hospitals won't let you in to visit at that point. So I told them to go to the parking lot where they could look up and see her room, and that's where we would pray together.

By this point, we found out that her weight had decreased to only eighty-five pounds. Doctors had made the prediction that at this rate, she would be dead by two o'clock in the morning.

Meanwhile, the man who called me and his wife had gotten into position within sight of the room and we prayed for the dying lady. Instantly, she was delivered and healed. It turns out that she had curses placed on her by Santeria and Voodoo witches while she was down in Jamaica. Those curses would have destroyed her life, but God stepped in through the prayer of His people.

That illustrates how important it can be to pray. Also, when you pray with others, you need to pray in one accord. When the saints agree in prayer, it adds so much power. The Holy Spirit even told me that for every person praying in accord with one another, the power increases by a magnitude of ten!

It becomes even more powerful as we understand that the root of all sickness and disease is a demon. Every sin people commit is from a demon and they do it because there is pressure put on them. Every person must come to the knowledge of the truth, because that is the only way to get free. Otherwise, you're left to depend on the doctors, and they can only do so much.

Let me say this: I am not opposed to doctors or to seeking medical help. Sometimes we've prayed to the best of our ability and seen no change. When that happens, it's sometimes necessary to go to the doctors to see what they can find out. Many times, they'll uncover information that helps you pray more effectively. Sometimes they can really help out. At the same time, believers can never lose sight of the fact that the physical is a reflection of the spiritual, not the other way around. If we're able to deal effectively with the spiritual root of sicknesses or diseases, we can see real healing and not just treatment. There's no condemnation for going to the doctor. It's just that the Great Physician is the better choice!

If you notice, most people who focus strictly on the natural eventually succumb to the disease, especially if it is terminal, but there are starting to be a growing number of people being healed and restored from even terminal diseases. For example, think of the man I mentioned earlier, named Wes, who was completely healed from diabetes.

For another example, when we had our third child, Carolyn had a lump building up on her neck. Our youngest son was about six months old when she went to the doctor, and he diagnosed it as cancer of the thyroid. Carolyn didn't understand what cancer was. She was totally naïve about it. The doctor told her she needed to come in the following Tuesday for surgery, and she responded that she couldn't do that. He replied that if she didn't come, she wouldn't live long enough for another appointment. Mind you, this was before we were Christians. In the end, she went in for the surgery, but even after the surgery, the doctor only gave her two months to live.

Of course, she is still alive and kicking to this day. But she did not allow the fear of cancer or the fear of dying to enter her mind. Even though they took out over three quarters of her thyroid gland, she still takes no medication whatsoever. Actually, neither one of us take any medications or vitamins at all. We just rely on the Holy Spirit to tell us what we need to pray, and we cast out demon spirits.

Even before we knew about prayer, we could see how it affected our lives. When we'd been married seven or eight months, our mobile home blew up with us in it. That's a very bad way to wake up at six o'clock on a Saturday. It's very rude. It blew Carolyn out of the home, and her hand literally burnt a place on the blanket on our bed and gave her third degree burns on her face, hands, and legs.

The doctors wrapped her up in bandages for six to eight

weeks. They were trying some experimental treatment on her. What they didn't know was that Carolyn had a praying grandmother. When they took those bandages off to start skin grafting, they discovered brand new skin. She has no scars and is just as pretty today as she was then.

We can barely comprehend all the wonderful things God is doing! He's even gone so far as to remove the curse that had been on women in childbirth since the days of Eve. When our daughters-in-law were getting ready to have their babies, we prayed with them and destroyed the curse of childbirth so they wouldn't go through the pain and suffering. As born-again Christians, they had the right to destroy those effects of the curse.

Then, after they had the babies, as soon as we could get to them, we did deliverance on the babies. We cast out the spirits of trauma, traumatized, traumatizer, and every spirit that entered them when they came through the birth canal and into this cold world. We've been very busy praying over our grandchildren this way, but it has caused all of the births to be so peaceful.

Another area to understand is that believers have authority over weather conditions. I first experienced this in 1983, when Carolyn and I were headed to Pampa, Texas, for a funeral. I had just gone off of flying status a few months earlier, so I understood weather conditions very well.

As we were driving, we saw three very large clouds, very disturbing to look at, off to the south and west of us. I could tell that they would end up meeting and crossing our path somewhere behind us. As we watched, those three clouds came together and formed a tornado a quarter of a mile wide at the base. I looked at it and sort of shrugged it off because I knew it would pass behind us and not get close to where we were.

All at once, supernaturally, my right hand flew off the steering wheel. I pointed at that cloud with two fingers and said, "In the name of Jesus I command you devils to come out of that cloud in Jesus name." It was like a thousand corkscrews came out of the cloud and within two or three seconds, there was no cloud whatsoever. It was just a clear blue sky.

After that we've dealt with many, many tornadoes coming our direction. One day, while I was working out at Tinker Air Force Base, a tornado was moving toward our home, and Carolyn went out in the yard and commanded that tornado to go north. Well, it did, and a lot of homes were destroyed in the Edmond area. One of the homes was completely wiped out – the only thing left was the floor. That happened to be the home of a pastor who had strongly opposed us.

This only goes to show that we have authority that most people have not tapped into as of yet. But if we understood what the Bible says, that would be a different story. What do believers have authority over? According to the Bible in Genesis 1:28, it is every living thing. So what are demons? Living things. What are angels? Living things. This kind of understanding changes the way you look at situations and how you pray. I hope that now, you'll begin to pray in the authority God has granted you in His Word.

I want to share one more very unique experience that happened to us in 1989. We were driving to Houston at about 5:20 in the afternoon. We were on Highway 45 headed south out of Dallas. The traffic was moving along at about seventy-five miles an hour, bumper to bumper. To my right was the concrete wall, and to my left, close enough I could have reached out my hand and touched it, was an eighteen wheeler hurtling along.

I had tried to put a little distance between my car and the one in front of me, but as soon as I did that, another car slid into that tight little space. We went probably two or three hundred yards down the highway and all at once, the car in front of me turned sideways. There was nowhere to go, and I never even let off the accelerator!

All at once, I just looked back and there was that car, still turned sideways, but it was behind us now on the highway. Obviously, we wondered what was going on. Later that evening, our middle son called and asked, "What was happening at 5:20 this afternoon?" He told us that at 5:20 the Holy Spirit had told him to pray quickly! So he prayed, and obviously his prayers worked.

I've wondered ever since whether God shrunk our vehicle so we could just pass through what little space there was or if we somehow went over that car. Maybe we went right through it? I know now, we went through it.

About a year or two ago, a person shared an experience with us that confirms it to me. The person was over in Germany for their child's wedding. They were in a Mercedes-Benz, and another car ran a stop sign. They hit the other car broadside. Then they actually went into the car and took that car with them for about a block's distance. The driver was looking right at them. Then they passed on through. There was not one bit of damage to either vehicle. It was a supernatural intervention on their behalf.

When I heard that, I knew that was exactly what happened to me. Those types of events have happened before, and they're going to be happening a lot more frequently than before. We need to be ready for them. We need to expect this type of miraculous intervention to increase as we really dig into prayer and the supernatural world.

God is not a respecter of persons, so I know that He will perform the same kind of wonders in your life. All it takes is for you to really believe Him, really obey Him, and pray like your life depends on it. You've probably figured this out by now, but it actually does depend on it.

Say Father

CHAPTER 15
A LIFESTYLE THAT DEMONSTRATES THE LOVE OF GOD

I believe the Holy Spirit is leading His people into a lifestyle of supernatural power, not just a lifestyle of occupying a pew. In fact, I'll go so far as to say that you'll encounter so much more of the Kingdom of God *outside* the church walls than you ever will within them.

Now that doesn't mean I'm against church or churches. We go to church because the Lord commanded us not to forsake the assembling of the saints (Hebrews 10:25). If the church is functioning correctly, the meetings of the church will prepare every saint to get out and minister the Gospel of Jesus Christ. The five-fold ministers – apostles, prophets, evangelists, pastors, and teachers (Ephesians 4:11-12) – will reproduce themselves in the church body, and every part will be edified, encouraged, and ready to go take on whatever comes their way. That's the ideal way a church should operate, anyway.

And on top of that training and sending out, when we come together as a body, Jesus likes to manifest Himself in our midst. We encounter His glory in a myriad of ways, we're transformed to better carry that glory to the world, and we take it out to show all those we encounter that Jesus is alive and He loves each and every one of them.

I'm encouraging you to stop seeing your Christian faith as a once-a-week practice, and start viewing it as an ongoing lifestyle. It's not a pond, it's a river of living water (John 7:37-39). It's a constant flow as you freely give what you've received from the Lord. And you'd better be ready at any given moment to demonstrate the reality of the Kingdom!

Once, I had been visiting a chiropractor because I had fallen off the roof. When I landed my ribs were dislocated from my spine, and the chiropractor was helping get my spine and ribs all back into alignment. About the time we pulled up to the office one day, the nurse came running out to us saying, "Hurry, hurry! There's a man in there manifesting!"

As we got into the office, it turned out to be a young man we knew. They asked us to take him into the X-ray room to do deliverance with him. As we started working with him, his eyes turned blood red, like two red balls stuck into his face. Then he levitated about a foot up out of his chair and just hovered there above it. It took us a while to get him all leveled out, but we did.

Now it wasn't like someone had told me on the way to the chiropractor that we'd be delivering someone when we got there. That was a complete surprise that got sprung on us at the last moment. So when the Bible says to be ready in season and out, that's not a joke! We need to be ready at all times, and the only way to remain constantly ready is through the baptism of the Holy Spirit. If you look back at the very beginning of the church, Jesus told His first disciples in the first chapter of Acts to remain in Jerusalem until they were endued with power. Chapter two describes the actual baptism of the Holy Spirit and the magnificent power released when that happened. The disciples were transformed from a leaderless group hiding in the upper room to a power-packed bunch in mere minutes. That's the same model for us today.

We need to remain in God's presence until He pours His Spirit out upon us to the point of overflow. We need to continually receive of the Holy Spirit, and as I may have mentioned a time or two throughout this book, we absolutely *must* rely on Him for everything we do. If we can get that down, we have a chance!

Furthermore, I really don't think we have a choice in the matter if we really intend to obey what Jesus told us. In Mark 16:15-19, He made His will perfectly clear: "*And he said unto them, Go ye into all the world, and preach the gospel to every creature. 16 He that believeth and is baptized shall be saved; but he that believeth not shall be damned. 17 And these signs shall follow them that believe; In my name shall they cast out devils; they shall speak with new tongues; 18 They shall take up serpents; and if they drink any deadly thing, it shall not hurt them; they shall lay hands on the sick, and they shall recover. 19 So then after the Lord had spoken unto them, he was received up into heaven, and sat on the right hand of God"* (KJV).

I use the King James here to show you that Jesus commanded His followers to go, preach the Gospel, and flow in the power of the Holy Spirit. Any time in Scripture that you see the word "shall," understand that this is legal, contractual language. It establishes an action as imperative or mandatory. In other words, it is not a request but a command. If we disobey His command, we are walking in disobedience, which is the spirit of witchcraft (1 Samuel 15:23).

However, Jesus didn't intend for that command to be done like a chore. It's really fun to demonstrate the goodness of God wherever we go. A good place to start is to simply share with people what Jesus has done for you. Don't get caught up trying to beat them up with the Bible! Instead, let them hear what amazing things the Lord has done in your life. That opens the door for the Holy Spirit to draw them to Jesus. Then, they begin to want what you have.

When they ask how to receive it, lead them through the sinner's prayer. Then cast out the demons that have been ruling them and operating in and through their lives. Pray to get them baptized in the Holy Spirit, and help them receive any healing they need. Then you can bring them to church!

Most people get this completely backwards. Psalm 1:5-6 says we're not even supposed to have sinners in the congregation. Yet Christians are trying to bring sinners into the church to get saved, which is causing a mixture that hinders the Holy Spirit from working as much as He could if the congregation consisted of Spirit-filled Christians only. As I've said, the church is the place we're supposed to be educated on how to minister the Gospel. Then we go out into the streets, businesses, and homes to get people saved, baptize them in the Holy Ghost, and delivered so we can bring them to church to be taught on how to do likewise.

After all, every person is commanded to minister the Gospel. It is not the pastor's job, or even the fivefold ministry's job per se, to get people saved. It is the job of every born-again believer to preach the Gospel.

The goal here is to be ready when the Lord presents you with opportunities to present people with the reality of the Living Word of God, Jesus Christ. He will draw them to you, and you get the opportunity to show them His love.

For example, recently we were at a restaurant and a waitress sat right down at our table and wanted to talk. Then, when we got ready to leave, she just wanted to hug all of us! Now that's not a normal activity for a waitress. So I told her, "Say, Father..." I led her in a simple little prayer, and afterward she was just elated. She grabbed me in a big old bear hug. But it just goes to show that people out there on the street have needs, and as the church, we are the hands and feet of the Lord Jesus going *out* to meet those needs.

Another time, I was getting my haircut at the barber shop. I just visited with the man who was cutting my hair, and when he was finished, he gave me a big old hug! Whenever love is reaching out of you, it's touching the lives of the people around you. Love is the key that opens the hearts so you can deal with the spiritual part of the people you encounter. If you do that, they can receive as well. That's what it looks like to give what you freely received.

We will be presented with opportunities every day to minister to somebody in such a way that will bring them closer to receiving the Lord. Perhaps you'll plant; maybe you'll water seeds someone else has sown. You might just be the one the Lord sent to harvest that soul into His Kingdom. But all of this comes from the power of the Holy Spirit. You can still be a Christian and go to Heaven without the baptism of the Holy Spirit, but you will lack the power to effectively minister the Gospel.

Unfortunately some Christians just don't want to hear that. For example, about a year and a half ago, a man I had been acquainted with had a son who started feeling suicidal. They called in the psychiatrist, but that wasn't helping. This father had talked to me just enough that he knew what I operate in, so he decided to bring his son to me.

We set up a meeting, and I immediately dealt with the spirits of suicide, premature death, and self murder. We cast those demons out, and the change was immediately noticeable. Now we're talking about a young man who had been to hospitals and had who knows how many tests done, but the minute those spirits came out of him, he said, "Dad, that's where the problem has been all along!"

I gave God glory for such a miraculous healing. The young man has been doing very well ever since, but his father still wants absolutely nothing to do with me because of what a lot of people view as "traditional" doctrine.

That's why we have to stay focused on the Word of God, not the doctrines of man.

So our job here is actually really simple. We continually allow the Holy Spirit to cleanse us from any evil operating in our lives, and that allows Him to draw people to us so we can minister to them in His power. I read in a book called the Archko Volume that Jesus never chased anyone down. Instead, He allowed the Holy Spirit to draw people to Him. The Holy Spirit quickened me that this was absolutely true, and that we ought to be the same way. You can look at the Gospels to confirm all of this, by the way. But if we are watchful and ready, the Holy Spirit will put people in our paths who need to be touched by the love of God.

Personally, I've had people tell me that when they get within three to four feet of me, they feel something like an electric current flowing through them. I don't feel anything, but the people tell me they feel it. I don't want to burst their bubble and tell them I'm not really different. But there will be a difference in God's people that others can visibly see. They'll know there's something they have to have. It's not that they merely desire to have it – they *have* to have it! We need to pray that the Lord would draw people to us like a magnet, such that they cannot stay away.

Unfortunately, there are so many people in the church today who are not living the truth of the Kingdom. So why would the people around these believers want to come to them for help? Therefore, it is essential to bring the knowledge of the truth into people's lives in such a way that the unbelievers are drawn to us instead of wanting to run from us!

One important part of that kind of life is to be sure that we remain in God's will. Something each and every person needs to consider is whether or not they are doing with their lives what God wants them to do. Carolyn and I never imagined what God would call us to do, but we sure did obey when God showed us. That's the only reason I can come up with for why God has allowed us to do all the amazing things we've done.

The tragic error we're making is that so many of us are telling young people they can be anything they want to be. That's simply not true. God actually has a plan for us that is all written out. He knows the plan already, and it's up to us to seek His revelation of it.

The Lord has been speaking through some international prophets about the scrolls He has written for every believer. When our spirit is sent from Heaven at the moment of conception, there is a scroll placed in us that outlines our life from conception all the way to death. I had never heard of that in my life, but the moment I heard it, my spirit man grabbed ahold of it. I knew that I knew that I knew that was true. Psalm 139:16 notes that all our days are written in God's book before they ever come to pass, so it lines up with the Bible as well.

The simple truth is that God has a plan for each one of us, and that plan is written on the scroll. We need to call up on the angels to bring us knowledge of that scroll. We need to ask the Holy Spirit to reveal that scroll to us. That's how we'll discover God's amazing plan for each and every one of us. He wants us to know it, but we won't know unless we ask.

Every person on Earth wonders, "What am I here for? What is my purpose? Who am I? What am I?" All kinds of questions like these circulate through people's minds, especially out there in the world. They have no idea why they were born. That's why there is so much confusion, so much drug and alcohol addiction, so many addictions to sex, and so much perversion. People simply don't know their purpose, and they don't feel that they're worthy of anything good or wonderful. So, if we have knowledge of what that scroll inside us says, then we have knowledge of hope and a future, something that is productive to humanity.

So let's just make this really practical. A good place for you to start if you truly want to live a supernatural lifestyle that demonstrates the love of God is to seek His will for your life. Are you in the job He wants for you? Do you live in the state or city where He has planted you? Have you done what He has called you to do? Ask the Holy Spirit for revelation and wisdom over every area of your life and follow what He says to you. I promise you, you won't be disappointed.

As you're going, stay grounded in the Word of God. Allow the Holy Spirit to guide you and teach you the deep things of God's heart. Equip yourself with the truth and refuse to compromise for anything less than the absolute best God has for you.

Dig into the ministry of the Holy Spirit. You can spend the rest of your life learning from Him and you'll barely scratch the surface of what He's capable of. But He will take you higher and further than you ever imagined. I haven't been disappointed yet, and I'm more than thirty years into my journey!

Purpose in your heart to become effective in deliverance ministry. Learn to protect yourself and your house from the schemes of the enemy. Be ready to help other people who have been trapped by the devil finally find the freedom they've yearned for. Work alongside the angels and the great Holy Ghost to see the Kingdom of Jesus manifest here on this earth. That's what we were created for, and there's no greater joy than to tear down hell and raise up the Kingdom of Heaven.

Listen to the Holy Spirit, obey Him without fail, and you'll never be the same. Neither will the people in your life. It may not be easy, but it is certainly worth it. And I pray that you will be led by the Holy Spirit into the plans God designed for you before time began. I pray that you will be anointed to fully accomplish God's perfect will for your life as He works through you to establish His Kingdom on the earth. Amen.

Say Father

APPENDIX
SAMPLE PRAYERS

Note: These prayers are intended to serve as a model. As I mentioned in the book, you cannot allow a formula to replace actively listening to the Holy Spirit. That's a recipe for disaster if there ever was one. These prayers will help you minister to yourself and to others in a variety of very common situations. However, there is not a substitute for being led by the Holy Spirit. Remember, always ask the Holy Spirit to teach you how to pray the effective, fervent prayers of a righteous man over any situation you're facing. He knows what to do, and He's the best teacher you could ask for!

Prayer for Salvation:

For this, begin by asking the person whether they truly want to receive Jesus as Lord and Savior and make Him the master of their lives. If they want to do that, then you can have them pray something like this: "Father, in the name of Jesus, I choose to receive Jesus as my personal Lord and Savior, and I choose to make Him my master. I repent for all my sins, and I ask Your forgiveness for every sin I've ever committed, in the name of Jesus. Father, I ask You to wash me from all unrighteousness and make me complete, in Jesus' mighty name."

The Holy Spirit may give you more to pray, depending on the person's personal situation or their level of knowledge. The key, as with all of the prayers, is to listen and hear what the Lord wants you to pray with and for that particular person. Trying to turn any prayer into a formula is a guaranteed way to fail, as I've noted before.

Prayer for Others to Get Saved:

Father, in the name of Jesus, I call on Michael, Your chief warring angel, to capture and sever the chords of communication between the controlling and ruling fallen angel that is over (name) and capture and remove that spirit permanently, in Jesus' name. I bind the demon spirits at work in (name) and command that they be bound, gagged, and paralyzed so they can no longer have an influence on (name) in the name of Jesus. Now, in Jesus' name, I dispatch the ministering angels to go to (name) and start ministering the Word of God in such a way that (name) can understand and bring people across his/her path who can teach him/her. In Jesus' name, I release the warring angels to surround and protect (name) from all evil assignments. Holy Spirit, I ask You to go to (name) and draw him/her with such love, conviction, and power that he/she can no longer refuse the Lord Jesus Christ, in Jesus' mighty name!

Prayer for Testing Spirits:

Father, in the name of Jesus, I address the spirit who said/told me _____. Do you call Jesus Christ Lord and do you worship and serve Him only? I command that spirit to answer me now, in Jesus' name.

A spirit from the Lord will testify that Jesus is its Lord and that it serves Him only. Silence, negative feelings, swearing, a definitive "no," or anything that is not a direct affirmation of Jesus as Lord indicates that the spirit is not from God and it should be dealt with immediately.

Prayer to Forgive Others and Destroy Ungodly Soul Ties:

Father, in Jesus name, I choose to forgive (name them specifically) for (name it specifically). It is my will, and I choose to forgive (name) in Jesus mighty name. Father, I also ask you to forgive (name) for (whatever it was), and to bless them with your best blessing, in the name of Jesus.

Now Father in the name of Jesus, I call upon Michael to take his sword and destroy all ungodly soul ties between (name) and me, and between me and (name). Michael, take your sword and destroy them now, in Jesus' mighty name!

Now, in the name of Jesus I command that the controlling and ruling spirits (over the person being forgiven) be cast out in Jesus' name. Holy Spirit, push them up and out of me. Michael, sack them up, jerk them out, and take them where Jesus has sent them, in Jesus' name.

Prayer for Returning Soul Fragments:

Father, in the name of Jesus, I call upon the ministering angels to return every fragment of (name's) soul left in (me/person you're praying for) back where they belong. I charge the mighty warring angels to escort the ministering angels as they return those soul fragments in Jesus' name. I also command every fragment of (my/person you're praying for) soul to be returned to (me/them), escorted by the ministering and warring angels in Jesus' name. Holy Spirit, I ask you to restore (my/person's) soul and make (me/them) whole and complete, in the name of Jesus. Thank You Lord for making (me/them) whole.

Prayer to Remove Transferring Spirits:

Father in the name of Jesus I command every demon spirit that has transferred from another person or location to (me/person) to be bound with the chains of Jesus. Holy Spirit I ask You to push them up. Michael, sack them all up and jerk them out of me in Jesus' mighty name!

Prayer to Cleanse the Home:

Father, in the name of Jesus, I call on the warring angels to capture and remove all demon spirits from my home, the closets, the rooms, the inner walls, the attics, the basements, under the floors, all around, above, and beneath my home. Clean out every part of it and remove those spirits, in Jesus' name! I charge the warring angels assigned to me to stand guard over my home and my entire property and protect all of it, in the name of Jesus. I invite the ministering angels to come and take up residence in my home and to minister to every person who enters. Lord, I pray a shield of Jesus over my home, and I coat that shield with the precious blood of Jesus, in Jesus' mighty name!

Prayer to Neutralize Poisons:

Father, in the name of Jesus, I command all poisons and all chemicals in my body to be neutralized and to pass immediately from me, in Jesus' mighty name.

Prayer Over Trauma:

Holy Spirit, I ask You in Jesus' name to reveal any trauma that has opened the door for the enemy to operate in, on, or through (my/person's) life. (Allow the Holy Spirit to reveal what He needs to reveal. Take your time and listen well.) Holy Spirit I thank You for revealing this trauma. I invite You to come and heal (me/person) from the trauma (I/person) suffered, and I thank You for the healing in the name of Jesus.
Now, Father, in Jesus' name, I bind every spirit of trauma, traumatized, traumatizer, along with every kindred spirit that works in or through them or that is tied to them. Holy Spirit, push them up and out of (me/person) now, in Jesus' name. Michael, I call on you to capture all of these spirits, bind them in the chains of Jesus, sack them up and jerk them out of (me/person) now, in Jesus' mighty name!

Prayer to Cast Out Spirits Common to Man:

Father in the name of Jesus, I bind every spirit of hurt, deep hurt, rejection, rejected, rejection in the womb, grief, sorrow and bitterness. I also bind every spirit kindred to these that operates with and through them and every spirit tied to them in Jesus' name. Holy Spirit, I ask You in Jesus' mighty name to push those spirits up and out of me now. Michael, bind them in the chains of Jesus, sack them up and pull them out of me, in Jesus' mighty name!
Note: Other spirits common to many people include anger, hate, murder, rage, vengeance, violence, vindictiveness and every spirit kindred to them that works with and through them, along with every spirit tied to them.

Prayer to Destroy Witchcraft:

Father, in the name of Jesus, I destroy all curses, every curse upon a curse, all hexes, vexes, spells, wishes, incantations, chants, charms, enchantments, all rites and rituals, all words spoken over, about, or against (me/person), all workings, and all generational and inherited curses. I destroy all of these back to their beginnings in Jesus' name. I dispatch the warring angels to capture ungodly words in the atmosphere and all ungodly written documents and destroy them back to the beginning, in the name of Jesus. Now, I destroy all shields, seals, oracles, circles, pyramids, veils and all such protective devices in Jesus' mighty name.

Prayer to Destroy Buddhist Monk Curse on American Troops in Vietnam War

Father, in Jesus' mighty name, I command all of the word curses spoken over me, about me, against me and my family by the Buddhist Monks in Vietnam be reversed back to the original sender seven-fold according to Psalm 109:16-20, and I now command the spirits that were sent to carry out the curses of Addictions, Vagabon, Poverty, Anger and Family Destroyer be bound with the chains of Jesus. I now destroy all of your legal rights to me and my family back to their beginnings; now I ask Holy Spirit to push these devils up, and Michael, I ask you to sack them up and jerk them out of me now, in Jesus' mighty name.

Our War Against Hurricane Gilbert

In late summer of 1988, a hurricane named Gilbert formed off of the northeastern coast of South America and set a northwesterly course toward the Yucatan Peninsula. As it was nearing the Yucatan Peninsula, it had a recorded speed of 199 miles per (mph) and as it was crossing the peninsula, the speed dropped below 160 mph, then accelerated again to 199 mph with a projected landfall near Brownsville, Texas, and projected wind velocity in excess of 200 mph. Hurricane Gilbert was expected to follow the coastline all the way to Florida.

When this hurricane started developing, I received a phone call from Vena Cullen and Betty Hord who lived in Houston, Texas, and they were praying with a group of intercessors against the storm. They asked my wife, Carolyn, and I if we would join with them and of course we agreed to do so. I then asked them how they were praying and what their strategy was. About the second day as we were praying, Carolyn said, "I'm seeing two eyes in the storm; the top one is offset from the one below, like there is one hurricane on top of the other." When I got off of the phone with Vena and Betty on either the third or fourth day of intercession, I asked the Lord how He wanted me to pray and His answer to me was, "My son, pray a shield of Jesus between the water and the winds, so the spirits of Poseidon, Leviathan, Neptune and (a fourth spirit I believe was Hercules), cannot rise up out of the waters and give strength and acceleration to the spirits of storms, hurricanes, tornadoes, high winds, destructive winds and killer winds." Then He said, "Dispatch Michael and the warring angels into the storm and capture all of the demon spirits to destroy the storm."

When I finished praying what the Lord told me to pray, I started praising Him for the awesome revelation He had just given me, and I also thanked Him for the 12,000 angels that He had sent to me to minister for me (Hebrews 1:13-14) and that they had done such a marvelous job ministering for me. The Holy Spirit immediately answered me back and told me, "you have access to the same number of angels that Jesus did when He went to the cross." (More than 12 legions or 72,000).

As I was trying to comprehend all that the Lord had just given to me, again the Lord spoke to me and said, "My son, pray My Word, Exodus 22:18, 'Thou shalt not suffer a witch to live.'" So I rather flippantly prayed, "Father, Your Word says in Exodus 22:18, 'Thou shalt not suffer a witch to live,' so I release Your Word to do its work according to Your will and as You direct by Your Spirit." Almost immediately, I had an open vision of five witches drop dead behind a stone sacrificial altar and another witch drop dead as she was doing dishes in her kitchen. I immediately started crying and I told the Lord, "I don't want to be responsible for people dying who have not had an opportunity to meet Jesus and make Him Savior, Lord and Master of their lives." The Holy Spirit immediately told me, "Only those who have committed the unpardonable sin or have hardened their heart so strong against the Lord that they will never receive Him will die and they need to be removed because they are a hindrance to My body."

When we were praying, we were asking for supernatural protection for all of God's people, that there would be no injuries or deaths, nor any damage to their homes or property.

On the morning of the fifth or sixth day, we heard on the TV news that the hurricane turned sharply into Mexico and quickly dissipated. That same afternoon, we received a phone call from Vena and she told us that the Lord had given one of the intercessors an open vision of three huge mountains between the east coast of Mexico where the storm made landfall and Monterrey. On top of each mountain, stood a huge warring angel and they were slapping the winds with the flat side of their swords and she said the winds were falling to the gorund like broken glass. The Lord told her that one angel represented Betty Hord, one represented Carolyn, and one represented Ken for their warfare.

Kenneth & Carolyn Howerton
RADAH Ministries, Inc.
105 Yukon Ave.
Yukon, OK
73099

The Analysis of the Human Personality

GOD OPERATES THROUGH THE SPIRIT	KING (THE BLOOD LINE OF JESUS)	SERVANT	SLAVE	SATAN OPERATES THROUGH THE BODY
	SPIRIT	**SOUL**	**BODY**	
	BORN AGAIN NATURE (Romans 14:17) • Righteousness, Peace, and Joy • Revelation • Communication • Intuition • Conscience ROYAL NATURE (Revelation 1:6) PRIESTLY NATURE	MIND • Intellect • Thinking • Evaluating EMOTIONS • Feeling • Desire • Mood WILL • Deciding • Volitions	TOUCH TASTE SMELL HEARING SIGHT	

NOTES:

1. There are five primary steps to demon possession, as follows:
   - Regression
   - Depression
   - Oppression
   - Obsession
   - Possession

2. MOST Christians fall within three categories. (sickness, disease, mental torment, poverty, etc.)

3. NO CHRISTIAN can be demon possessed.

4. The first three steps are self explanatory; however, demon obsession occurs when demons have taken over the soul (mind, will, & emotions). Demon possession occurs when the spirit of man has been taken over and the demons have complete control of the person's spirit, soul, and body.

5. The word "shall," as used in the King James translation, is a contract word meaning that there are no other options, as in Mark 16:17, and all other Scriptures where the word shall is used.

6. The "Blood Line of Jesus" surrounds the spirit of man, but does not surround the soul or the body.

Ungodly Soul Ties

Earth & the Three Heavens

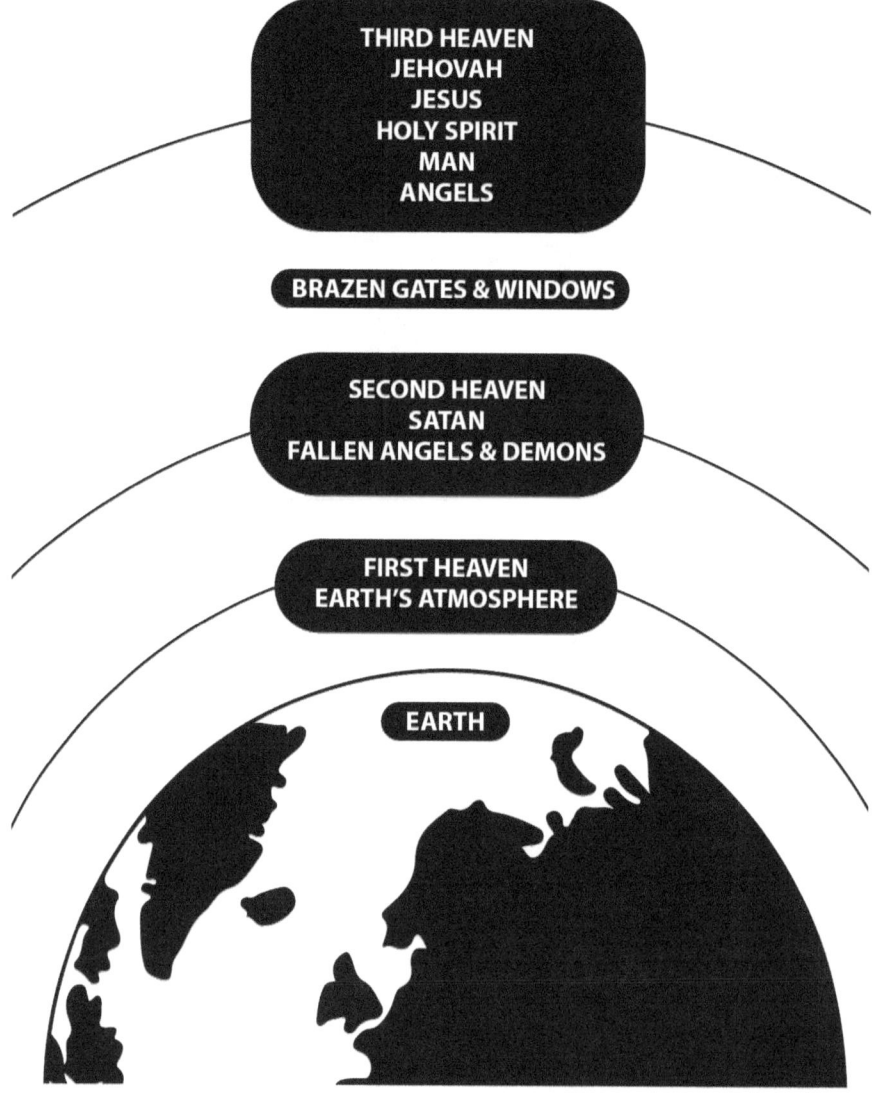

Satan's Organizational Chart

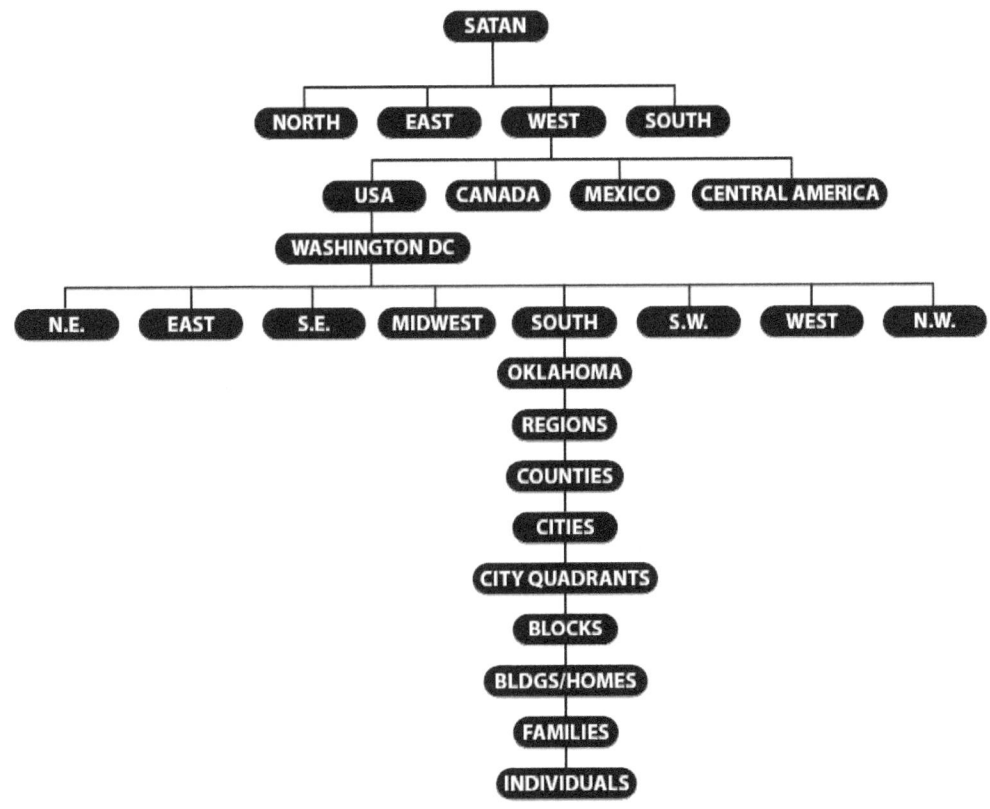

ABOUT THE AUTHOR

Ken and Carolyn Howerton are a true Apostolic father and mother in the faith of our Lord Jesus Christ. They move powerfully with the Father's heart of love to save, heal, and deliver those who are in need. They both have a passion to see the fullness of God in Christ Jesus made manifest in the church as He establishes His Kingdom on Earth. They love teaching, equipping, and serving the Bride of Jesus through the Word of God and the Spirit of Revelation. They rejoice and have great joy in their wonderful marriage, children and grandchildren, and reside in Oklahoma.

GARDENPUBLISHINGCO.COM

    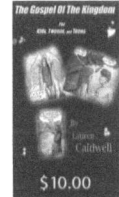 

$16.00 — $15.00 — $11.95 — $11.95 — $10.00 — $15.99

$15.99 — $44.99 — $15.99 — $15.00 — $10.00 — $10.00

  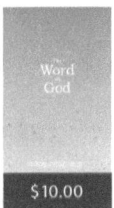  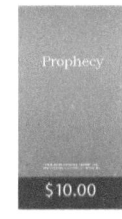 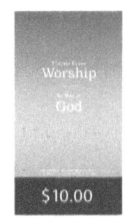

$10.00 — $10.00 — $10.00 — $10.00 — $10.00 — $10.00

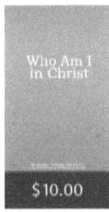   

$10.00 — $10.00 — $10.00 — $10.00

www.ingramcontent.com/pod-product-compliance
Lightning Source LLC
Chambersburg PA
CBHW020426010526
44118CB00010B/440